I HOPE GOD'S PROMISES
COME TO PASS BEFORE
MY BODY PARTS
GO SOUTH

I HOPE GOD'S PROMISES COME TO PASS BEFORE MY BODY PARTS GO SOUTH

Cathy Lechner

I Hope God's Promises Come to Pass Before My Body Parts Go South
by Cathy Lechner
Published by Creation House
Strang Communications Company
600 Rinehart Road
Lake Mary, Florida 32746
Web site: http://www.creationhouse.com

Unless otherwise noted, all Scripture quotations are from the King James Version.

Scripture quotations marked MSG are from THE MESSAGE. Copyright © 1993, 1994, 1995. Used by permission of NavPress Publishing Group.

Scripture quotations marked NKJV are from the New King James Version of the Bible. Copyright © 1979, 1980, 1982 by Thomas Nelson Inc., publishers. Used by permission.

Scripture quotations marked AMP are from the Amplified Bible. Old Testament copyright © 1965, 1987 by the Zondervan Corporation. The Amplified New Testament copyright © 1954, 1958, 1987 by the Lockman Foundation. Used by permission.

Scripture quotations marked NIV are from the Holy Bible, New International Version. Copyright © 1973, 1978, 1984, International Bible Society. Used by permission.

Scripture quotations marked NAS are from the New American Standard Bible. Copyright © 1960, 1962, 1963, 1968, 1971, 1972, 1973, 1975, 1977 by the Lockman Foundation. Used by permission.

ISBN: 0-7394-0380-X

Printed in the United States of America

Our six (and counting) beautiful children. You are the consummate and glorious answer to my years of tears and travail!

Jerusha Rose, Hannah Ruth, Gabriel Levi,
Samuel Josiah, Abagael Elisha, and
Lydia Danielle

AND TO:

Erin Colleen Yancey, my armorbearer, my right hand, my Ruth, my secretary, my daughter in the Lord, and my sister in Christ. You are my "Forever Friend."

Acknowledgments

I have a lot of acknowledgments to make for this book. If you have no chance of being acknowledged, then you probably won't even read this. Shame on you.

I need to thank the makers of chocolate-covered raisins. They have seen me through some very troubling times. Also, my poodle Beau, who gives me enormous joy and a great deal of sermon material.

To Stephen and Joy Strang, my friends and co-laborers. I know you will disagree because of your genuine humility, but I owe much to you. You have my respect, my love, and my loyalty. You also have my royalty check. Thank you!

To my publisher, Tom Freiling, who has patiently sat at many restaurant-table meetings, smiling and drumming his fingers on the table the day before my deadline. You stayed sweet, even when you wondered if there would ever eventually be a manuscript. The Lord has mighty plans for you.

To Rob Clyde—someone who really understands me. It can't be that easy to explain these titles to bookstore owners. You're my favorite too.

To my editor, Alyse Lounsberry, who believed in what I had to say and encouraged me to say it—and did a great deal of hand-holding through this book. May God use us as a Paul and Barnabas together for the building of His kingdom.

To my pastors, Wiley and Jeana Tomlinson and Bob and Mary Louise Bailey, who seem to never tire of loving and pastoring me. Thanks also to my church family at New Covenant Ministries in Jacksonville and my covenant friends at New Life and Church of the Messiah.

To my ever-patient, always-loving, and hard-working parents, Clive and Rose Rothert, who help me get through deadlines and much tribulation.

To Michael, Terry, Elisabeth, Abagail, and Mariel Brantley. It is certainly written about you: "A friend loveth at all times."

To Cyndi and Dwayne Carrillo. My, was I blessed when you came from the West!

My love and appreciation to Daniel Robinson, who has made my children a ministry.

To my darling, praying grandmother, Ruth Rothert, whose prayers are more precious to me than gold.

To Mark and Judy Schubert, my burden-bearers.

To Terry Ward, thank you for your selfless love shown by quietly ministering to me.

To Rick Godwin, who has absolutely no idea who I am, but whose principles and teachings over the years have lifted me to a new level. Your willingness to be a line-crosser made me one too. (Please don't sue me for using your teaching material for ten years.)

To Eric and Lynn Jones, who are not only on our covenant staff but are our covenant friends as well.

To Trudy Cooper and Ellen Ludlam, who faithfully serve.

Finally, I wish to thank the two most important people in my life—my Lord Jesus, whose voice is what I live for and whose "well done" is all I seek, and my husband, Randi. You are my rock, my reason, and my best friend. And yes, I finally know after twenty-one years that you would do anything for me. Thank you for pushing me to pursue the best God has for me.

CONTENTS

INTRODUCTION

GOD is crazy about you. He is absolutely, totally, smitten in love with you! Right now He is thinking about ways to bless you. Do you believe that? You need to. It is one of the keys crucial to seeing your promises birthed.

I really don't think there could be anything quite as frustrating as being filled with promises, hopes, and desires, and never seeing them come to pass.

This year has been a warfare year for me. You see, in one hand I hold promises of answers to prayers given to me by my loving, awesome God. In the other hand I hold a sword, and I've been busy doing the battle necessary to actually come into those very promises. Each step forward has been hard-won ground. The victories, of course, are sweet, sweet, sweet. The reward has been—Himself! He has given me His own precious presence. The anointing has increased. I really don't want to tell you about my losses. There were times I tossed my sword away and shouted, "Forget it! It can't possibly be worth it!" And there were times I all but wore out my all-time favorites, "Why me?" and "Why *not* me?"

During such moments I can see that God can still love and use me in spite of my weak will and feeble failures. It's all part of the adventure, I guess. It gives me hope.

So once again, dear reader, come along on a wonderful journey with me. And since we have to do it anyway, let's have a good time. My motto this year has become, "If we must suffer before the answer comes, then we are going to celebrate a lot while we are waiting."

Now, which way to the cake and ice cream? Oh yes, I forgot—I am doing the low-fat thing . . . so which way to the cake and sorbet?

—*Cathy Lechner*
Jacksonville, Florida

One

LORD OF THE IMPOSSIBLE

DRAGGING one suitcase with my free arm and kicking my garment bag down the hotel corridor, I clenched the room key between my teeth. I know that is unsanitary, but, traveling as much as I do, I simply must block out the image of my mother pointing her finger at me and saying, "Cathy Lee, get that filthy thing out of your mouth. You don't know where it's been."

As I dropped the last of my bags in the middle of the hotel-room floor, I heard the Spirit of God speak to me. His voice was so clear—not audible, but loud and plain—and this is what He said: "Cathy, you are living in the *possible.*"

I was in Rock Hill, South Carolina, standing in a hotel room, feeling tired, wrinkled, and yucky from traveling all day, and I was not prepared to hear the voice of God. It isn't that I haven't heard Him speak before. In fact, my whole ministry is centered on hearing from my Savior's heart. Usually, I am waiting on Him, or at least listening to a praise tape when He speaks.

When I heard, "Cathy, you are living in the possible," I fell to my knees in the middle of the floor, surrounded by my unpacked bags. I lifted my hands to heaven and began crying out to God in my most official, spiritual voice.

"Thank You, Lord. Thank You for Your love and affirmation," I cried to Him.

"This is not a compliment; it's a rebuke!" the Lord replied.

Excuse me! I couldn't believe what I was hearing. Immediately I began to argue my case in my mind—a case I thought to be quite excellent—hoping God would over-hear.

On the Road Again . . .

I TRAVEL every weekend, leaving behind my husband and children in order to obey God's mandate to teach the Word. I write books and put myself under deadline pressure so that others might be encouraged. You have heard me mention numerous times that my husband, Randi, and I adopted five babies, saving them from the enemy's hand. So I felt entitled to argue, *I do at least twice as much for the kingdom as most people I know!*

But God sees things differently. "Daughter, living in the possible is where most of My people live. You can stay there if you want to. But if you desire those things that you have seen by My Spirit, prophesied by My Spirit, and if you desire to be a part of My great End-Time move, then you must come out of the possible and live where I am."

"But I don't know where that is, Lord."

"It is in the impossible. As long as you stay in the possible, *you* are lord. But if you are willing to step out here where I am, I am Lord of the impossible."

I was broken. I was caught. When anyone tells you that they heard God speak, it becomes highly subjective—you know, raised eyebrows and visions of the Hale-Bopp comet. I have even questioned the conversations other Christians claim they have had with God. When He spoke to me, He wasn't angry. When He spoke, His voice was full of mercy and compassion. Even though His words contained a rebuke, God was *nice* to me! What a novel idea.

About four hours passed as I wept there on that spot in room #103 of that hotel in Rock Hill. During that time the Lord lovingly dealt with me, showing me areas of doubt and unbelief hidden beneath the surface of why I was so careful to stay within the realm of the possible.

Even though my current level of faith and obedience was, I thought, a stretch, I had become comfortable there. As long as no one got a major disease, the car didn't break down, and the household income remained the same, I could handle it. I had everything under control. That's life in the realm of the possible. You pretty much don't need to call on God because you have it all together. You do not even need much faith because you are just maintaining.

On any given day a circumstance or situation will come along that will force you out of your comfort zone and thrust you into the uncharted waters of the unknown. It is there that you become acquainted with the Lord of the impossible.

Don't try to swim back to shore; it won't work. Embrace change with joy. (It wouldn't hurt to have some Raisinets to help you through it either.)

THERE'S A STORM A'COMIN'

I HAVE found in my own life that God does not introduce a new thought because He has nothing better to do. He introduces a new thought because it is preparation for the next level that He desires to take me to.

The conference over, I flew home on Sunday, not realizing that my life and walk with God would be changed forever. Even this ministry would take a new direction because of the dealings of God that weekend.

Early Monday morning my daughter and I were at the athletic club working out. (Just a side note for you readers who are now being hit with pangs of guilt about never exercising: Personally, I believe exercise to be a demonic plot to force us to put on ridiculous-looking red lycra outfits, buy overpriced yet fashionable footwear, fix our hair, put on make-up, then sit down and watch thirty minutes of *Body by Jake* on the Family Channel.) For myself, I prefer gym equipment that makes you look better without having to actually *do* anything. My first free visit to the facilities was cut short when I interrupted the instructor who was giving a demonstration of the life cycle to ask if they had something less sweaty, like a Jacuzzi. She rolled her eyes at me, took one look at my sagging, cellulite-ridden thighs and hindquarters, and took me directly to the weight room. She handed me a half-pound weight and asked me to lift it. I sneered, thinking, *I can lift two three-year-old kids while balancing a whining, clinging, two-year-old who is hanging on to my leg as I try to walk and still manage to pull a roast out of the oven while holding the phone to my ear with my shoulder and jaw!*

This skinny little child rolling her eyes at me was no match for me. I took the weight and, glaring directly back at her, asked if they had any tanning beds.

I'll Say, "Maybe, Lord"

THAT MONDAY morning, after the Lord had dealt with me all weekend, I was at work on the ten-degree incline bench. I had just dropped the weights after a rousing rendition of two when the Holy Spirit spoke to me again.

"Cathy, they are going to call you this morning from the adoption agency. They have a mixed-race infant girl for you. My hand is on her, and I have a great destiny for this child. I desire for you and Randi to adopt her and raise her for My kingdom. Call her name *Lydia.*"

Lying on that bench in my help-me-Jesus-I'm-so-ugly

clothes, sweat was dripping down my face. (Of course, the gym's air conditioner picked that day to break down.) I began to argue with God.

"But, Lord, we have no more room; our house was too small two children ago. I have no baby stuff because I gave it all away. We really don't have the finances to pay for another child. Lord, You know I'm recuperating from surgery and my strength is gone. It just is not convenient at all. Really, it's not!"

Do you know what the Lord said in answer to my argument? *Nothing!* Zip, zilch, not another word. You see, God opens an opportunity for us to reach into the realm of impossibilities—but He won't force us to go.

Driving home from the gym, I shared what I felt the Lord had spoken to me with my then nineteen-year-old daughter Jerusha. I poured out my heart to her concerning the Lord's dealings with me, hastily explained the difference between the possible and impossible realms, and finally told her about the new baby girl God said He was going to send.

She stared at me, totally unmoved, and answered, "Surely, Mom, you are *not* thinking about obeying God! Please, Mother."

"Well, I don't want to get leprosy or have a leg fall off or get sucked up by a great fish while I'm showering," I lamented.

My daughter's only response was, "Oh, me!"

"I Guess It Must Have Been God"

No SOONER had I changed clothes, poured a cup of coffee for myself, and settled down in my comfortable recliner when the phone rang. Jerusha answered the call. I looked up and saw her standing at my bedroom door with a look of disbelief on her face.

"First of all, Mom, you're good. You are *very* good. Second, you're scary. You are *very scary*. Who will ever want to date me? It's the adoption agency." She said all this as she handed me the phone.

A baby girl had been born over the weekend. While God was dealing with me in that hotel room in Rock Hill, the mother was in labor. A home was needed for the infant. Would Randi and I be interested in adopting a biracial baby girl?

I told the agency I would have to call back. I sat there, stunned. Having God speak to you about stepping out in faith and then actually having to do it are two entirely different things.

It's really funny. Just the day before I was singing a little chorus with these words: "I'll say yes, yes, yes. I'll say yes, yes, yes. I'll say yes, Lord, to Your will, Lord. I'll say yes, yes, yes." Now I was singing, "I'll say maybe, maybe, maybe."

Having been married for twenty-one years, I have learned there are some things you do not do. One is walking in and announcing to your husband, "Oh, man of Godeth, the Lordeth hath toldeth me that you arteth to thence taketh a baby of the female gender and raiseth her upeth forthwith."

No, no, no, no. You don't do that. At least it has never worked for me. That afternoon I shared with my husband about the phone call and this new "opportunity" that God had opened up.

Adopting a baby is not like buying a cantaloupe or a new car. You can't change your mind and trade it. Randi and I knew that. He asked me if we had any baby stuff. *No.* Did we have any money to do this? No, except for the one hundred and thirty dollars in store coupons and a secret hidden twenty-dollar bill that I kept in my underwear drawer. "Our house is too small, no room for another baby. We need to hear from God," he said.

I remember thinking at the time, *We have no room, no time, no money, no strength, or energy. Yup, sounds just like God.* When it is the most inconvenient and when you are just starting to find your comfort zone, God says, "It's time to stretch again."

CONGRATULATIONS—IT'S A GIRL!

THE NEXT morning Randi and I sat down to talk. I asked, "What did God say?"

His reply was simple: "God said that He had already spoken to you, and we are to do what He told you to do." I was excited and scared at the same time.

That very afternoon found us on an airplane on our way to pick up our precious new baby girl. Everyone was throwing out his or her favorite names. I said nothing. We had pretty much used up all the really good Bible names. The only ones left were the obscure, ugly names like Hoglah and Zephunigliad, one of which probably means "the cattle are dead."

Our then three-year-old Hannah wanted to be a part of it all, so she piped up with, "Let's call her 'Jumanji,'" which, of course, is the name of some magical popular film.

"What about Lydia?" There; I said it. Everything God had spoken to me prophetically about this child was unfolding. I wondered if Mary, the mother of Jesus, or Elisabeth, the mother of John the evangelist, ever felt as overwhelmed as I did at that moment. And so, Lydia Danielle became a Lechner. It was love at first sight,

Beloved, God sovereignly provided a bed and clothes— not just nice things, but exquisite dresses, booties, and blankets.

WHERE DID EVERYONE GO?

LESS THAN a week later, I was on an airplane, headed north for a three-day conference with Lydia in my arms. We had no sooner checked into the hotel when I noticed that I already had a message waiting. My husband had called and said it was urgent.

I phoned home immediately and was told by Randi that our attorney needed five thousand dollars by the close of business that day in order to cover all medical and legal expenses Lydia's birth had incurred. Not even a week old and she was already in debt.

Obviously, we didn't have the money. I started to panic. Randi asked me what we should do. I guess he thought, *She's the one who heard from God. Surely He's given her the rest of the plan.* It was suggested that we write a post-dated check. I didn't think writing a post-dated check to an attorney was such a good idea, especially since we had no way of covering it. I could sense that a big argument was brewing between us, so we said good-bye with my last words being, "What can they do to us *now?* Are they going to come up here and repossess the baby?"

As soon as I replaced the receiver on the hook, I could feel discouragement and depression settling in. A cloud of hopelessness was rapidly replacing the joy and excitement that I had been walking in all week.

My first inclination was to cry out, "Oh, God, why did You leave me? I trusted You and said yes."

Sitting on the edge of the bed in still another hotel room in yet another town, the gentle Spirit of God now nudged me: "Cathy, having stepped over into the impossible with Me, are you now going back to the possible with your problem?"

"I guess not, Lord. But the time for the miracle is only four hours away, and I do not see any possible way for You to do it in the time You have left."

"Is there anything *you* could possibly do to bring in the money right now?"

"No, Lord."

"In the realm of the impossible, *I* rule and reign. Trust Me."

With that, the burning bush departed. (Not really. However, I verbally pushed off despair and discouragement and set myself to bring the Word and ministry that weekend.)

THE LORD OF THE IMPOSSIBLE

WE HAD a glorious time in His presence during that whole conference. I never mentioned my "problem" to anyone. It was during the last Sunday morning service that the pastor asked me to bring Lydia to the platform so that he and the elders could pray for her. He handed me an envelope and said it was a gift for the baby. I was thinking, *A twenty-dollar gift certificate to Sears,* which would have been a welcome gift.

We went to the pastor's office after the service, and he asked me if I had had an opportunity to look in the envelope. I told him I hadn't as yet. This is what he told me: "Cathy, all during last night the Holy Spirit kept speaking to me to bless Lydia. It was so strong that I finally had to call the elders to hear if they were in agreement. They were. We need land to build our new sanctuary, and we are planting this seed in Lydia for our new building. Open the envelope."

In the envelope was a check for five thousand dollars. I fell to the floor weeping. I wept not only because God had met our need, but in shame for my lack of trust in the Lord of the impossible.

God knew the plan from the beginning. He had already seen the baby, prepared a family, and covered the financial part. How glorious is our King!

IF YOUR DREAM DOESN'T SCARE YOU, IT'S NOT BIG ENOUGH!

NOT EVERYONE who found out that we had taken another baby had the same revelation. Even family members made statements like, "You need your heads examined!" Not everyone is called to do what Randi and I have been called to do. In fact, most people are glad *not* to have the calling to adopt little children. However, *everyone* is called to walk in the impossible.

When I was a little girl, one of my favorite television programs was *Mission: Impossible*. Every week I would watch this little band of crack secret agents whose expertise qualified them to continually be thrust into impossible situations. Every week I would watch as they barely escaped with their lives, one close call following another.

Watching someone else do it on television, or even listening to someone's testimony, is enough to make us shake our heads and say, "Better you than me." Another profound statement is: "That's as close as it gets." We can remain distant, safely ensconced in our little world of the possible. Or we can step over into the impossible realm, where it's really scary.

I'm praying that, just as it was no accident that this book has come into your hands, by the time you finish reading it you will accept the challenge to move over into the rollercoaster realm of the impossible.

TWO

THE IMPENDING BIRTH OF YOUR PROMISES

As a child I heard the following text thundered many times from various pulpits: "Where there is no vision, the people perish" (Prov. 29:18). What the pastor really meant was, "It's building-fund Sunday, so let's get the little red thermometer hanging on the church wall to go up, up, up." That is, unless it was Mission Sunday. Then it meant, "You spoiled, fat Christians need to give, because thousands of people are waiting to hear the gospel, and if you don't give, they won't hear, and they are going to die and go to hell, and it will be your fault!"

What Proverbs 29:18 actually means is this: "Without a vision, a dream, a prophecy, or a revelation, My people will die." God is saying, "You need something *bigger* than yourself to live for."

I remember hearing a story on television about a woman who was blind for years and came to a healing miracle crusade. The man of God prayed for her, and she was instantly healed. Everyone was wild with joy and praise, including the man of God. The healed woman just stood there. She was asked if she had anything to say. She said, "God told me if I would come here and have you pray for me, I would see again. It took me six days to get here because we came three thousand miles by car. AND GOD DID IT!"

This woman had a vision, a word, a revelation. That was what had kept her going. "Unrelenting disappointment leaves you heartsick; but a sudden good break can turn life around" (Prov. 13:11, MSG).

Do you need a break? It's not going to be found at the fast-food place, my beloved. My prayer for you is that, as you read this chapter, new hope, new vision, and new revelation will rise up within you for your situation, whatever it may be.

God Desires to Restore Your Hope

I LOVE to prophesy and speak a word of hope confirming or unlocking the hidden dream within God's people. However, *getting* the word is the easy part; *walking out* that promise to its fulfillment is the hard part.

Anyone can receive a word. All you have to do is show up at the conference, church, or prophetic meeting. But… it takes time and patience to bring it to completion.

Conception, pregnancy, and delivery are the perfect examples of receiving, nurturing, and fulfilling the word of the Lord in your life. Let's draw a few parallels along these lines.

Prenatal care is the most perfect and proper environment necessary in order for your promises to be birthed on the earth. I hear so many Christians say, "Sister, just put that promise on the shelf, and if it's of God it will come to pass." NO! You can no more put a promise or prophecy on the shelf and expect it to live than you can put a human fetus on a shelf and expect it to live. If you just walked away and left your promise on the shelf, you would suffer a spiritual miscarriage.

The human fetus derives life from his or her mother. It takes proper feeding, nurturing, and then monthly—and eventually weekly—checkups from the specialist. So it is with the promise: It requires our regular attention and prayerful nurturing.

A pregnant woman begins to see her body take strange forms. It stretches in ways she thinks are humanly impossible. So it is with promise in the Spirit: The ordeal of *expansion* must be endured.

Now, I confess that I like channel-surfing; it's so educational—especially when I occasionally land on The Learning Channel. I realize that in some of these programs they often show you things that you are better off not knowing. Take, for example, the "You and Your Liposuction" special I once watched from start to finish, glued to the tube in rapt fascination. They showed a flabby woman who must have been paid millions of dollars to expose what most of us pay big money to cover up. She was lying on a table, marked up like a side of beef on a steakhouse placemat.

The team of doctors proceeded to shove a long, skinny hose into her "problem area" (and not very gently, I might add). A droning machine that sounded a lot like a vacuum cleaner began to suck out her fat. That is not even the gross part. They put the fat into a mayonnaise jar, reversed the switch, and pumped it right back into her cheeks and lips!

I began to laugh as I watched the yellow fat accumulate inside that mayonnaise jar. That poor woman just *thought* she was sneaking that Twinkie in the middle of the night. She had no idea it would eventually show up on national television inside a used mayo jar!

Don't Miss Your Day of Conception

THERE I was again, in front of the television, channel-surfing, when I happened upon a program on The Learning

Channel on the topic of fertility. An expert in obstetrics was providing the commentary. Of course, I thought I knew just about all there was to know about pregnancy, having been pregnant once myself. As it turned out, there was a lot my physical education teacher left out of my ninth-grade "girls only" health class.

The TV doctor explained that during a woman's monthly cycle, there are just two days when she can become pregnant. (He began to utter a bunch of highly technical medical terminology that you and I as nonprofessionals could never begin to remotely understand. What he meant was, the woman's body fluid begins to do the dance of the seven veils, or something like that.) The other twenty-eight to thirty-five days even her own body fluid is resisting the conception of an egg. However, everything changes during those two days.

Out of those two days, there are actually only *two hours* when the highest rate of fertility is achieved. Of course, those of you who have thirteen or fourteen kids might not believe that. The point I am making is this: *Don't miss the day of your conception.* The Word of God in you is a seed of life. His precious Holy Spirit comes to fertilize and impregnate you with new life. Proverbs 30:15–16 tells us that one of the things that is never satisfied is the barren womb. It's the same in the Spirit realm. It is so frustrating to get word after word, promise after promise, and never see impregnation and implantation of the seed.

A female child is born complete with all the eggs she will ever have need of during her lifetime. Randi and I have four unmarried daughters. So each of our daughters has the *ability* to become pregnant but not the *capability* to become pregnant, since they have no husbands.

Many believers are that way. They have great destinies awaiting them. Within them is a whole lifetime of seed to be fertilized, nurtured, and sown. But they sit through meeting after meeting and service after service, coping with spiritual headaches, never allowing the Holy Spirit to bring forth life through them. That prophetic word is a seed of life! That seed is powerful. It contains spiritual DNA!

THE WORD OF LIFE

I WAS ministering the Word in Australia when I was drawn to a young couple sitting halfway back in the sanctuary. I stopped preaching, and, sensing an overwhelming feeling of the Father's love for them, I gave them a prophetic word. The main content of this prophecy was that even though they had lost a son, God was going to give them *many* children. He would bring these children forth from China, Romania, and even Australia. The husband began to sob uncontrollably. He and his wife fell to the floor and began to cry, "Yes, Lord! Yes, Lord!"

Shortly after returning home, I received a letter from this precious couple. Enclosed was a picture of their baby—the one that had died. However, the letter was filled with excitement and anticipation because they had a heart for orphans. The word of the Lord spoken to them had given life to their vision.

You see, the prophetic word speaks death to one season and life to the next. Very often we receive a promise from the Lord and our circumstances cry out just the opposite, contradicting the promise. (This is also why I have an unlisted telephone number!) Promise in the presence of contradiction inevitably creates a kind of spiritual discomfort.

What do you do? Do not abort the discomfort.

One day a woman stopped me in the mall and said, "Cathy, you gave me a word from the Lord that I would conceive and bear a son. The doctor told me it was impossible, but I'm *pregnant.*" I rejoiced with her and congratulated her. She went on to tell me that she had no symptoms, no morning sickness, no swelling, and no back pain. I told her that was wonderful and asked her how far along she was. "Two weeks," she proudly announced. The smile on my face froze. I wasn't about to speak a negative word of doubt or unbelief and rain on her parade. But from experience I knew some things she didn't. *Think, brain, think,* I commanded, while trying to find the right words to say. "Well, isn't that nice—only eight-and-a-half months to go." It was the best I could do.

One of the things that pregnant women begin to notice before their bellies ever begin to swell is the small, subtle changes. Many women know they're pregnant before the test ever verifies it. The small changes in their bodies are the seed's way of making its presence known. Some women have so much going on at the same time that it might be two or three months before it occurs to them that they might be pregnant. It doesn't really matter, because the end result is the same—the seed brings change. Everything in your life changes, and if you are not ready for change, then you are not ready for the word of the Lord. It also brings transformation.

Pregnancy Causes Discomfort

WHEN YOU discover that you are pregnant, the enemy will assault and bombard you with doubt, accusations, and questions about your ability to bring forth life. That alone will bring discomfort. Then there are the physical discomforts: morning sickness, swelling, aches, pains. Ugh!

Some women testify that the best they ever felt or looked was when they were pregnant. I would like to find these women and torture them. (Not really!) I just happened to have one of those pregnancies that had me throwing up for nine full months. I was miserable. I didn't have morning sickness; I had full-blown, twenty-four-hours-a-day, I-must-be-carrying-an-alien sickness.

The ladies in our church prayed for me. They tried to cast things out of me, into me, cut something off me, and even accuse me. Then, when they were through travailing in prayer, I threw up. I remember one precious woman, a mother in the group, who gave me this advice that I will

never forget: "Cathy, in a few months it will all be over."
She was right. As simple as that statement was, somehow it
gave me peace.

Over and over I have witnessed the power of the
prophetic word. I know what one word of hope can do
when whispered into the total darkness of the defeat and
depression the enemy tries to bring. God's transforming
word can bring order out of chaos and joy out of grief.

CAN WE TALK?

SOME LADIES love to sit around the table after a lovely luncheon of snooty ladies' food. They eat stuff like poached
skin of baby eel on toast points with a semi-glaze of
weatherproof shellac and fresh watercress on the side. I'll
take a milkshake with that. All but one of these women
have had children the old-fashioned way—in the back of a
wagon train with a bullet in their teeth, screaming whilst the
menfolk were outside doing man things and spitting.

The poor girl who has not had the experience of child-
birth is two months pregnant with her first. One of the more
seasoned luncheon ladies starts the conversation with this
seemingly trivial comment as she munches on her poached
eel, using her best Scarlett O'Hara drawl: "Is this your first
baby?"

"Yes, ma'am," the little unsuspecting gal answers sheep-
ishly.

Suddenly, the women exchange knowing glances around
the table. The sharks move in; the smell of blood is in the
air.

"Well, let me tell you about *my* labor! Bubba, he was my
first. He had so much hair, I had heartburn, and was in
labor three-and-a-half months. Many were the times I
wished I were dead. Then my second one, Jimmy Joe—
well, he came breech. Came out sideways, then went back
in. Would you believe his nose came out and the nurse tied
a scarlet lasso around it? They ended up slicing me open

and pulling him out. He weighed almost thirteen pounds." The ladies are all watching the helpless victim to see if her bottom lip has begun to quiver yet.

Of course, after hearing all nine ladies talk about their various degrees of pain (each worse than the last), the young woman asks, "How old is Bubba?", expecting to hear about his impending third birthday.

"Let's see, he'll be fifty-four come March, the same number as my stretch marks. But don't worry, dear, the Lord will help you." The ladies of the luncheon all add their amens, satisfied with a job well done.

Spiritual pregnancy and natural pregnancy have a lot in common. But one thing is for sure: While the end results are essentially the same, every pregnancy affects you differently. You can walk through a particular situation, apply some spiritual principles, and then BOOM! The answer comes. The very next day, week, or month, along comes another challenge and you respond the same way. You pray, stand, rebuke, sow a seed, and BAM!—nothing changes. Why? New levels bring new devils. Fresh revelation brings greater tribulation.

Being determined to follow through at any cost brings you into the second trimester, or second stage, of spiritual pregnancy, which is:

CARRYING THE PROMISE

THE SECOND trimester of a pregnancy is fairly routine but somewhat boring. You're too fat for your jeans, but you look ridiculous in maternity clothes. Everyone has advice for you, but it seems the promise is a long way off. You walk through the baby section at the department store, lovingly touching and oohing and aahing at all the wonderful and clever assortment of designer wear for infants. You look at the price tags and scream. You startle your mother, and so you tell her that you are not in labor, just in shock. A tiny sleeper that your baby will only wear once and grow out of within minutes is the same price you paid for your car.

It is the same way in the Spirit. You are full of anticipation and hope that the coming promise brings. You begin to realize that there is a hefty price tag on your new dream. The gospel is free, but it is *not* cheap. Don't quit now. Many lose their vision during this time. They become bored, tired, and even frightened at the cost of the expanded dream.

Please allow me to share some principles of the Word that I have learned from others who were pregnant before me.

I heard a gentleman by the name of Bernard Jordan make this profound statement:

> Don't share your dreams with half-brothers because everyone will not celebrate your dreams.

How many times have we come away from a serious time in prayer, or after having been in a glorious hour of praise, or perhaps after a sweet drive to work praying in the Spirit, only to blurt out to a friend or coworker about our wonderful experience. They snicker, sneer, and become ambivalent.

POP! That was the sound of my balloon. The really, really precious treasures I have from the Lord I have hidden in my heart. Some things are just too wonderful and holy to share. Somehow, relating them to others for approval or advice or just for the telling cheapens and waters down the experience. In addition to that, I have dreams that are so big many would laugh, and their doubt could sow doubt in me and cause me to lose confidence in my experience with the Lord.

RULE #1: PLAN FOR ADVERSITY

IT IS *you* who must persevere. Many precious believers want someone else to assume the responsibility for them and to take on their fight. They want the privilege of going to a dear saint and getting him or her to fight Satan on their behalf. If you always depend on others, you will become a spiritual parasite.

I do not like hard times. Someone once asked me if I thought Christians would have to go through the Tribulation. I laughed and told them I have already been through eleven tribulations. Don't despise adversity; it's the adversity that brings growth. Seeds do not mature until they come up *through* the ground.

I will admit that this next revelation will not cause you to stagger with the wealth of wisdom contained in it. I didn't even have to fast and pray for thirty minutes to obtain this truth. If you can grab hold of this principle now, it will be a sword in your hand to defend you and your household later:

> Discouragement is the most dangerous and most effective tool of the enemy.

Simple, plain, vanilla discouragement, according to Bernard Jordan, is what the enemy uses most often to neutralize Christians. Hopelessness will try to temporarily obstruct your vision. Prophecy is God speaking to your potential. When God speaks to you, He is not only speaking to you, but to your seed.

Another simple truth that I learned the hard way (the hard way simply meaning finally learning after doing it wrong so many times) is this: *The person who receives the prophecy is not the same person who fulfills it.*

Young Joseph possessed great dreams from God. The path to Pharaoh's court led him through prison. The boastful, immature Joseph we read about in Genesis 37:7 is a far cry from the Joseph in Genesis 45:14–15. By now a broken, humble, tender servant of God, Joseph was finally able to live out the lofty dreams given to him as a young boy.

You can't imagine how many times I cried out, "Lord, if this desire is not from You, then please take it from me! It seems You are not in a hurry to bring it to pass, so remove the longing." God did not remove the longing because it truly was from Him. I just didn't understand that He had not yet worked the character of His Son into my life. He knew that for all my snorting, stomping, sniveling, and complaining He couldn't allow me to give birth in the second trimester.

It is important to know that the time of waiting is also the time of preparation. The force of our confession is made manifest through our words. Our words are not magic bullets or mantras. It is not the "power of positive thinking" that brings fulfillment; it is the power of life in our tongues as we continually declare, *"I can make it. I will make it!"*

Remember you are never too old, too young, too single, too divorced, too black or white, too male or female, short, tall, fat, or skinny to be blessed! You are entering into the realm where miracles are not a once-a-year oddity but a common occurrence.

THIRD TRIMESTER—LABOR BEGINS

SOMETIMES THE very thing I desire makes me most miserable—just like my pregnancy.

On my first visit to the doctor after learning I was pregnant, I remember sitting on the edge of the examination table and freezing. I was dressed in a paper gown. (I wore two . . . one with the slit in front and one with the slit in back because I forgot what the nurse told me to do.)

The doctor came into the room holding my chart in his hand. Suddenly, I began to pour out my fears to this total stranger in a starched white lab coat.

"Doctor, I'm just so afraid I won't know when I go into labor. I'll just be busy vacuuming the carpet, and my baby will drop out, and I'll suck her up in the sweeper and have to rip it open with my teeth and rinse her off...." On and on I rattled. The doctor just looked down his nose over his glasses, staring at me in what I am sure was disbelief.

Smiling, he crossed his arms and said, "Mrs. Lechner, don't worry, *you'll know!*" He wrote something on my chart—probably, "She's nuts."

He then assigned me a due date. Now I don't mean to complain, but I personally think the assigning of a "due date" is grossly unfair. Mine was May 8, but by mid-April the doctor said I "could go anytime." May 8 came and went. God's way is that He will tell you "what" He is going to do, but rarely "how and when." He just assigns you a due "season." But when labor begins, you have absolutely no doubt this is it; *you are in labor.* The good doctor was right. *I knew.*

Labor Demands All of Your Attention

THE TIME of discomfort signals the imminent manifestation of the blessing of God. In other words, the more it hurts, the closer you are. That's the good news.

Randi and I took Lamaze classes to prepare for the birth of our daughter. That's where I discovered that lying on the floor, nestled in a pillow with my husband's arms wrapped around me, and "playing" labor (knowing that an hour later I'm going to be at Denny's eating a bacon cheeseburger) is a far different thing than actually *being in labor.*

In spite of what Hollywood says, you don't look and feel so great during or immediately after giving birth. Exhaustion may very well precede birthing, so don't despair when it comes.

Labor is work, and you must work your prophecy. In Lamaze class they taught us to concentrate and keep breathing when the pain became unbearable. We must keep the Word of God before our eyes, remembering always that the Holy One of Israel, who is our husband, will not forsake His bride as we bring forth His life in us.

CONQUER THE FEAR OF LABOR

DON'T CONFORM to comfort and take the road less painful. Conquer your fear of labor by leaning into the pain. Remember, fear is *F*alse *E*vidence *A*ppearing *R*eal.

I used to believe that if I could just have the perfect combination of words with enough faith to finally get God's attention, He would say, "Finally, Cathy, you got the perfect combination of words, faith, and timing, so I'm going to answer your prayer."

If anything, I have learned that God may have a hidden agenda for my miracle, and just because I don't understand does not mean that He has forgotten me. Just because I have not seen any visible results does not mean He has said, *No.*

When you are challenged with a vision that would promote God's kingdom, think of yourself as a chosen disciple.

If your life is anything like mine, at any one time I may be pregnant with four or five different visions, all at different stages, all quite impossible for me to fulfill in my own might and strength. But God is Lord of the impossible.

Take the risk God is asking you to take. Step out of the possible and join me out here in the realm of the impossible. Sure, it's scary out here. But believe me when I say, "It's worth it!"

Three

I'M POSITIVE GOD JUST WANTED TO KNOW IF I WAS WILLING

I was in the bathroom doing bathroom stuff when a woman with a flushed face caught me. "Cathy, wait a minute. I've just *got* to tell you." Words tumbled out of her faster than my brain (or hers) could keep up with.

"You've given me several prophecies over the past few years that God said I would have a baby. No one believed me, especially my husband. For ten years I have held on to that promise."

"And...," I tried to help her along. The running water was not helping the situation any. I had a reason for ducking into the restroom before the service began.

"I'm pregnant! Six weeks. We are ecstatic ... well, I am, but my husband is zombie-like. Praise God!"

We rejoiced and wept. (Water needs to be released one way or another.) We praised God for fulfilling His promise to His covenant daughter.

On the drive home, I began to think about my friend. For ten years she waited for her promise. She was living with a husband she dearly loved, but he didn't have a clue about how to see the impossible-seeming promises of God fulfilled.

It would have been so easy for this woman to yield to depression or to blame her husband for not standing with her. She even could have allowed the enemy to use the passage of time to wear her down. I knew she had become discouraged on many occasions. What was it, then, that had brought her through? Which divine principles gave her the strength to persevere? Was there a secret she stumbled onto that triggered something in God that finally made Him move on her behalf?

I cried, "Tell me, Lord—please tell me what I need to do!" I began to write as He spoke to me and said, "Many Christians never partake of the things that I have for them *because they are not willing to wait.*"

Randi and I were so excited because everywhere we go we are hearing testimonies recounting promises and prophecies that were received and are now coming to pass. God is truly moving quickly to fulfill His Word.

Yet, there are so many others who have a dream or vision in their hearts. These dreams and visions seem so impossible and have been so long in coming that they are weary and ready to give up.

To achieve the highest reward in a Christian life, we must stay on the road that takes us through the valley of patience. Many never persist all the way through the valley to their reward.

> And now I want each of you to extend that same intensity toward a full-bodied hope. Keep at it until the finish. Don't drag your feet. Be like those who stay the course with committed faith and then get everything promised to them.
>
> When God made his promise to Abraham, he

backed it to the hilt, putting his own reputation on the line. He said, "I promise that I'll bless you with everything I have—bless and bless and bless!" Abraham stuck it out and got everything that had been promised to him.

—HEBREWS 6:12–15, MSG

INSTAMATIC FAITH

WE LIVE in a time when we want things instantly. To *our* modern mindset, any element of waiting seems equal to inefficiency, laziness, or even worse. Remember, this is a generation accustomed to having it all—right now.

Do you realize that you could live your entire life from your car? You can drive through fast-food restaurants, banks, laundry and drycleaning establishments, get your doughnuts and coffee through a drive-through window, and finish off the week with a drive-in church.

I must admit, that concept really appeals to me. I could just stay in my muumuu—you know, the really comfortable one with the ripped-out armpit, the one I can't bring myself to throw away because I bonded with it three years ago. I get just as impatient as anybody, and I like to have things right now too. My worst nightmare is having to wait at the drive-through at Taco Bell with five screaming children. I also get very annoyed when I am put on hold. How about that computerized voice that gives you twenty minutes of selections?

No wonder that when God introduces us to an element of waiting our minds and flesh scramble to find something to "do" while waiting.

I hate standing in line. For this reason, I am loath to eat at cafeteria-style restaurants. My husband loves their fried fish almondine, so we can compromise and eat dinner at three o'clock in the afternoon. I will do almost anything to avoid "the dreaded line."

The exception is when I see that very unadmirable trait in

someone else. That's when I become righteously indignant. After a morning service I often ask for anyone in the congregation who needs a miraculous intervention from God to come forward for prayer. I have seen people shove each other out of the way so they could be first in the prayer line, then grab their purse immediately after being prayed for and run out the door. Of course, they would be forced to wait for a few minutes more if they received a "word"— and wanted to take home a copy of the tape.

> Don't overlook the obvious here, friends. With God, one day is as a thousand years, a thousand years is as a day. God isn't late with his promise as some measure lateness.
>
> —2 PETER 3:8–9, MSG

Patience is an active force! God is patient, but He is not inactive!

PATIENCE IS NOT ...

I REALIZE that when you start talking about patience, people heave a sigh and have visions of long lines at Disney or of being covered with cobwebs while waiting. Let me tell you what patience *is not,* and I believe you will be encouraged.

Patience is not aimless activity. How many dear saints do you know who have said, "I'm just waiting on the Lord"? The interpretation of that statement is, "He may move ... and then again, He may not. Therefore, I am not getting my expectations up so I won't be disappointed."

Patience is certainly not denial. It only *seems* as though you've been waiting fifty years for God to save your wretched family. We give up so easily. My mother used to tell me in that soothing mother-voice all mothers use, "When God closes a door, He always opens a window." She said it when I didn't make the cheerleading squad, didn't get the lead in a play, was stood up by a boyfriend, or went through a church split. I wanted to throw myself on the bed and cry, "I don't want a window! Why can't He open a door? What if I can't fit through the window?" She understood then, as I do now with my children, that God has a plan—if only I can just wait.

I don't use that old door/window cliché with my children. I tell them, "Yeah, I know. Sometimes it seems life stinks, and it's not fair. I wish I could wave my hand and say, 'You will never have to hurt while you're waiting.' But do you know what? It doesn't matter where you are because God knows where you're going, and where you're going is *good!*"

Patience is not timidity. Nor is it being a doormat or a pushover for people to step on so they can get ahead. In fact, patience is a strength. Anyone who can exercise it demonstrates a self-control and assurance that only the strongest in character possess.

Patience is not that "gritting your teeth while you wait" attitude. Even my dentist has verified the fact that this is not a good thing to do. In addition, that finger-tapping, foot-stomping counterfeit that some call *patience* is actually "controlled impatience."

Patience is not passivity or slothfulness.

PATIENT AND PERSISTENT

THEN WHAT exactly is patience? We must understand patience for exactly what it is, since without it we will never obtain the promise!

Patience means "the capacity of calm endurance." In other words, a patient person is someone who is capable of bearing delay. That, no doubt, just wiped out about two-thirds of us.

It gives a visual description of someone who is long-suffering with a lack of anxiety—a person who is voluntarily controlling himself and his feelings. It means perseverance.

Perseverance is "adherence to a course of action, belief,

or purpose without giving way." It is being persistent. And persistence is a steady, continuous plodding forward toward a goal with no faltering or turning aside or stopping to take a break.

Oh, dear, excuse me; I'll be right back. I need some Raisinets. I'll be with you as soon as I lick the chocolate off my fingers so that I can keep writing.

Patience is a calm endurance that comes from understanding. It's when we can say, "Hey! Relax! God is in control."

I'll be honest with you, my dear readers. Those of you who know me personally will agree with me that at times I have absolutely no idea what in the world I am doing. Surprise!

I love my husband, and I love my children; but because I love my Lord I can press on. After spending time alone with my Lord, I rise up and press on.

When we become impatient, our faith begins to waver. That's when we start to allow circumstances to steer us. We have fits and starts and begin to lose momentum. Maybe 90 percent of our battle is just being able to endure to the end.

> Do you see what this means—all these pioneers who blazed the way, all these veterans cheering us on? It means we'd better get on with it. Strip down, start running—and never quit!
>
> —HEBREWS 12:1, MSG

The story is told of a man who took his son fishing. The father and his son loaded up their fishing poles and took along a bucket of water filled with minnows to use as bait. After several hours of fishing without even a single bite, the boy tired of his rod and took a plastic cup and began to dip it into the bucket. Pulling out a minnow, he proudly showed his dad his "catch." When he returned home, his mom asked the boy if he caught anything. "Oh, yes," he replied. "Minnows in a cup."

For some believers, minnows in a cup are good enough.

They have no patience to hang in there for the really big catch.

To be patient is to wait—wait for God to move. And have you ever noticed that He seems to be in no particular hurry? God does not perform for us like a magician who snaps his fingers and causes things to happen. To wait patiently for an answer from God is a process—a wonderful, loving, scary, trying process. The one who goes into the valley of patience is not the same person who comes out.

That Old "P" Word!

FARMERS UNDERSTAND patience. They put the seed in the ground, bury it, walk away, and leave it. A farmer knows that a seed needs time to grow. Impatience—the attempt to harvest it too soon—will cause the seedling to die. It's the same with the seed in your heart. (And to think that I used to believe that all those fruits and vegetables just appeared from nowhere on the shelves at the supermarket!)

One of my favorite scripture verses, one that has sustained me many times, is Hebrews 10:23–24.

> Let's keep a firm grip on the promises that keep us going. He always keeps his word. Let's see how inventive we can be in encouraging love and helping out.
>
> —MSG

It is imperative to have patience and persistence if your dreams and visions are to be fulfilled. When they are challenged by the complexities of life, only patience and persistence will enable you to avoid becoming angry or discouraged.

A pastor once said, "The lack of patience always has a price, and its price is always higher than its opposite cost." Unfortunately, there are consequences of impatience. Most importantly, lack of patience causes you not to inherit the promises of God.

Here are some *characteristics that signal impatience:*

- *Indecision*—A lack of a sense of direction; starting something, then stopping.
- *Procrastination*—Always planning to do something but never actually beginning; not willing to do the "little" things God shows us while we are waiting for something "big" to do.
- *Neglecting to respond to ideas*—Being afraid that if we move forward, we will miss the perfect will of God; choosing to ignore the Holy Spirit's gentle promptings that just might contain the catalyst for God's blessing or someone's salvation.
- *Lack of organized planning*—Chaos is not the plan of the Holy Spirit. Contrary to what some believe, we can be led by the Spirit and still be organized. We have a family joke at our house that says, "When all else fails, read the directions." This came from many years of assembling toys the wrong way the night before Christmas.
- *Compromise*—Satan, through Pharaoh, offered Moses compromise after compromise when God called Israel out of Egypt. "It's almost the same thing." "Just leave your children." "Leave your cattle here." "Leave, but don't go very far." Moses held out for the promise. But Abraham said, "I want the promise—all of it—and I want it now!" What he got was Ishmael.
- *Daydreaming*—This is the opposite of faith. We wistfully hope and dream of something better, but "wishing doesn't make it so." Faith, on the other hand, is based on the Word of almighty God, who cannot lie.

How to Develop Patience

WE MUST realize that patience does not come automatically. We must:

1. *Line up what we are doing and thinking with the plumbline of God's Word.* (See Hebrews 10:35.)
2. *Get rid of sin.* Sin hampers progress. Sin will quench the flow of faith and patience. Sin stops the promises from working. (See Romans 6:12–18.)
3. *Lay aside any weight or encumbrance.* In other words, discard anything in our lives that does not promote obedience and fellowship with God. (See Hebrews 12:1.)
4. *Say no to fear.* Fear causes many Christians to become impatient. Fear of criticism causes many to procrastinate because they are afraid of what people might say. People who criticize or slander us can actually be used by God to develop a more Christlike character in us. (See Job 3:20; Romans 5:3.)
5. *Exercise our will.* Over and over the psalmist says, " . . . I *will* pray . . . I *will* obey . . . I *will* worship." He shows us that, in spite of every negative circumstance arrayed against us, we may follow his example and by force of will do the right thing. (See Psalm 18:3; 39:1; 54:6; 86:12.)
6. *Know what we want.* Our first response to this is probably, "I know what I want." Listening to many Christians' prayers has caused me to realize that we often pray (and think) in generalities, like, "Lord, *do* something!" What? If we are not specific in our faith and prayers, just how will we know when the Lord answers our prayers? (See 1 John 5:14–15.)
7. *Get informed.* The faithfulness of God and the

reality of His promises are revealed through His Word. The Holy Spirit will then have something He can use in us to create a tenacious grip on His promises. (See Proverbs 24:3–4; Habakkuk 2:2.)

8. *Meditate on our plan.* No problem can be solved without thinking on it. When we bring the presence of the Lord into our thinking and planning, it will block out negative and discouraging thoughts brought by the enemy. (See James 1:6–7.)

9. *Allow others to help.* There is wisdom in numbers and encouragement in sharing. Help others. Nothing is so putrid as a stagnant pool of water. Like the Dead Sea in Israel where no living thing exists or grows in or around it, so is a life all wrapped up in itself. (See Proverbs 11:14.)

10. *Stand firm.* The apostle Paul gives us the answer to the question: "I've done everything I can think of to do, prayed every prayer, believed with every fiber of my being, so now what do I do?" The answer is simple: "Having done all, stand." (See Ephesians 6:13.)

Stand!

Four

IF YOU HAD STOPPED AND ASKED FOR DIRECTIONS, WE WOULD HAVE BEEN THERE BY NOW

D ON'T you just hate stories that start out with someone telling you, in a very serious tone, "Now, back when I was your age..."? Then the person telling the story groans on and on about how he had to go to school twenty miles in the snow, on foot, dragging his camel in tow, barefoot, under the glow of the kerosene lantern, just him and Abraham Lincoln, blah, blah, blah. By then, you've turned this person off because, frankly, you don't care.

But I think that if we had just listened to some of these stories, we would have avoided many pitfalls.

I am a simple person. I just want to know what to do and how to do it. If someone could just tell me that, then I could get out of *where I'm at* and get on to *where God wants me to be.* That's all I need. In this chapter I'll talk about where I'm at and where God wants me to be—and I might even throw in a few "when I was a child" stories.

Don't cover your ears. The Holy Spirit is watching.

In Numbers 31:1–2 we read, "The Lord said to Moses, Avenge the Israelites on the Midianites; afterward you shall be gathered to your [departed] people" (AMP).

In dealing with the subject of seeing our promises come to pass, there simply must be a story about Moses and the children of Israel. The Israelites will certainly be the lifetime example to every Christian of how stupid we can be sometimes. God had given the children of Israel a promise and said, "You're going to go in and possess the land."

FORTY YEARS OF WANDERING

IN YOUR first Sunday school class you were told that forty years or so before the Israelites crossed the Jordan River into the Promised Land, twelve spies were sent into the Promised Land, and, rather than coming back and talking about the wealth of the land, all but two of the spies talked on and on about the many *impossibilities* of possessing the land. Because of the unbelief of the people, the Israelites displeased God, and He rendered swift judgment. He told them that the unbelieving generation would die in the wilderness. A journey that should have taken a year would stretch into forty, and God would take the next generation into the land, once their unbelieving parents had passed away.

I cannot think of a more horrible judgment than having to wait for a long time for something that should have taken a short time. There are principles, signposts, and guideposts in the Word that the Spirit of the Lord has given to us. If we will hear and pay attention, we can shorten our time in the wilderness.

Forty years had passed, and it was finally the next generation. Moses was getting ready to take the children of Israel across Jordan and release them to the land of their destiny. However, before he did, the Lord said that a great battle had yet to be fought. The Lord instructed the Israelites to avenge themselves on the Midianites.

We have a great vision and a promise that God has uniquely given to us. Contained in that promise are many little battles that we must fight in order to possess the bigger dream. This was the last battle of Moses' life. Had it been in today's society that God asked us to fight this last battle before He took us home, some of us would cry out, "But, God, *why should I do it?* I'm too old. There is nothing in it for me." But Moses knew that standing with others helps us come through to our own Promised Land—a truth God is revealing to His children even today.

In reading chapter 31 you will find that the battle against the Midianites was a very bloody battle. It was a hard fight. The children of Israel made many mistakes. They brought much spoil back to Moses, including some of the Midianites. God's instructions about dealing with them were both specific and harsh.

Moses and Eleazar the priest told the men of Israel they could not let the women live who were not virgins. The Israelites were commanded to kill the women. Then they were commanded to kill the male children.

I know you're probably thinking, *Cathy, what is the point you are trying to make?* I am emphasizing the fact that it was a long, bloody battle. Then, following the battle, according to Levitical law, the children of Israel had to sanctify and purify themselves. They were also required to offer sacrifices.

To recap, the Israelites fought a battle, there was much killing, they took the spoil, and afterward there were great sacrifices. And by *sacrifices* I don't mean just writing out a couple of checks. Ancient Jewish sacrifices were very involved processes.

Promised Land Straight Ahead!

It was finally finished. Sacrifices were made; offerings were given. We read in Numbers 32:1: "Now the sons of Reuben and of Gad had a very great multitude of cattle; and they saw the land of Jazer and the land of Gilead [on the east side of the Jordan], and behold, the place was one for cattle" (AMP).

Where did they get all the cattle? Reuben and Gad got the cattle from the spoils of war. In other words, they were blessed and walking in the blessings of God. They were on the east side of Jordan, and they saw that the lands they had just conquered—the lands of Gilead and Jazer—were lands suitable for cattle. Then this wonderful idea occurred to them: The sons of Reuben and Gad came to Moses and said, "All this land that we have just taken from the Midianites is a land for cattle. And you aren't going to believe this, Moses. *We have cattle."* See what they were leading up to? They approached Moses and said, "If we have found favor in your sight, let this land be given to your servants for a possession and *do not take us over the Jordan."*

I have shared in previous chapters about the difference between living in the possible and living in the realm of the impossible. For the children of Israel, the east side of the Jordan was the possible side. They were on the east side. And they wanted to stay there. Why? Because they had conquered it. It was already done. They had cattle, and so they appealed to Moses to let them stay where they were.

In order to fully appreciate the lesson and receive the memorial that God wants to give us, which will save us many headaches and get us into our promise faster, let's take a closer look at the tribes of Reuben and Gad.

JACOB'S BOYS

BEFORE HIS death Jacob, Reuben's father, spoke over Reuben and told him he would not excel. Reuben had already lost the preeminence and the right of being the firstborn before Jacob died because he slept with his father's concubine. Reuben tried to take a shortcut to the blessing. He tried to take a shortcut to receive what would have come to him if only he had waited in patience. By telling him that he would not excel, Jacob was saying that Reuben did not have a spirit of excellence. Thus, the Reubenites were distinguished as those who lacked excellence.

The tribe of Gad represented those who would always settle for less. They came short of the glory of God. Gad had a maverick spirit. The Gadites were nomads, wanderers. It is where we get the word *gadabout*. It means someone who can't stay still, a gadfly who flits from one place to another.

Therefore we have Reuben who did not have a spirit of excellence and Gad who was a nomad and a wanderer. These two came before Moses and said, "Let us stay on the east side of the Jordan."

The problem with that is that God had already said, "I want you on the *west side.*" The west side was the Promised Land.

I know there have been times in my life where the battles have been fierce and ferocious. I had a part of the blessing and would have been glad to settle for Jazer and Gilead, but God wanted to take me to Jericho. *Jericho* means "my sweet place in life."

Reuben and Gad said to Moses and the priest, "If we have found favor in your sight..." That smacks of religious, false humility, and they were clothed in it. I can almost hear the quiver in their voices: "If we have found favor in your sight..."

This is a new day, beloved. A new generation. Reuben and Gad were of the new generation. But Reuben and Gad said they did not want to go on. They wanted to stay where they were. They had proof that God was with them because they had the blessing. Still, they were willing to settle and insisted, "Don't take us over Jordan."

"Let's Go In!"

THE HOLY Spirit spoke to me out of this portion of scripture and said, "Cathy, I'm going to show you three reasons, three attacks of the enemy, that will keep my people from having the best of the land and from having the best that I have for them."

Something I have never been able to understand is why there are some people who do not seem to want God's best. My attitude is, *I am not going to bother putting on my pantyhose and showing up for church if it's not going to be great or awesome.*

When I was a child, we sang some of the most horrible, depressing songs. "Just give me a cabin in the corner of Glory Land." Who wants to live in a cabin?

Another one is, "Just build my mansion next door to Jesus." That's not good enough for me! I want my mansion to be located in Jacksonville, Florida. When I get to heaven, I am not going to sit around in a recliner with a remote control in one hand. God is preparing me to rule and reign. He's preparing you too.

Yet there are always those who appear to be content right where they are, without ever fulfilling the promise. Reuben and Gad were content without fulfilling the promise.

Many do not want to pay the price for God's best. They are content with what they have. They are satisfied with the possible. Reuben and Gad were content with the possible. They were content with camping over on the east side instead of crossing over into God's promise.

TIRED? GET OVER IT!

WHAT WAS the first principle that kept Reuben and Gad from possessing the best God had? They had come through the desert, fought a bloody battle, had purified themselves from the dead, and had made great sacrifices. They had acquired much cattle as spoil for all that effort.

The first principle is that Reuben and Gad were *too tired.* Everywhere I go I hear the same thing: "I'm tired! I'm tired!"

Sweetheart, *everyone I know is tired.* Everyone is weary. When asked how he dealt with a twenty-four-hour revival in Brownsville, Florida, three services a day, seven days a week, evangelist Steve Hill answered, "I get used to being tired."

My friend, *tiredness will keep you from having God's best.*

I was in a hotel room between services at a conference where I was the speaker. As I was channel-surfing, trying to find something to encourage me, I came across a program that was filled with people singing heaven songs . . . death songs. As the cameras panned the congregation, little ladies were taking hankies from their watchbands where they had tucked them away, and they were dabbing their eyes as they wept and sang. The more I listened, the more I became frustrated. The more frustrated I became, the more I paced the floor.

In despair I cried out, "God, why aren't these people already dead? They have been singing and prophesying *death songs* for forty years!"

My precious mother who was sitting on the bed in the hotel room dabbed her teary eyes too. She said, "Now, honey, don't make fun of them! Those songs really bless my soul!"

There are some people who live for heaven, but they don't live for destiny. So shake off that tiredness. Get over it! Or the enemy will use tiredness to keep you on the east side.

This plan of Reuben's and Gad's did not fly with Moses. He could not believe his ears. Moses knew the brothers were going to be in serious trouble with God if they did not help the other ten tribes fulfill the vision. Moses knew that it was going to take all twelve tribes to get across Jordan and conquer the land.

I can just imagine Moses with his hands on his hips, screaming at Reuben and Gad, saying, "Shall your brethren go to war while you sit here on your blessed assurance?" I'm sure that he went on a tirade against the tribes of

Reuben and Gad. He surely must have said, "We did this before, but not again! I put up with this once, but I am not putting up with it again."

In Numbers 32:14–15, Moses culminated by telling the brothers, "And behold, you are risen up in your father's stead, a brood of sinful men, to increase still more the fierce anger of the Lord against Israel. For if you turn from following Him, He will again abandon them in the wilderness, and you will destroy all this people" (AMP).

The worst sin of Reuben and Gad was that they weren't making decisions that impacted only themselves. Their selfish decisions would also impact everyone else. Moses said, "If you don't go in with the rest of us, you will be responsible for destroying all these other people."

How many times have we seen Reuben and Gad in our own churches? Their greatest sin is that they cannot get with the program. They begin to poison others against the leadership. To justify their unbelief or laziness they discourage others in the congregation or in the family, or even in a work situation, and cause them to settle for less instead of going on for the best.

Reuben and Gad asked for a sidebar. After talking it over among themselves, they returned to Moses and told him, "All right. We will do this. We will go over and help our brothers establish the land. However, we want to build sheepfolds and houses on the east side for our children and leave them on this side. Then we will cross over with you. We have decided that our inheritance has fallen to us on the east side of Jordan."

That was the saddest statement they could have made. In one moment they made a choice that would rob an eternal destiny for their children's children. With that statement they chose for their children and their children's children not to have the blessing of God.

Here is the part where I told you that you were forbidden to cover your eyes and ears. Growing up in a preacher's home, we did not have two- or three-day conferences. We had two- and three-week revivals. My father never asked us if we would *like* to go to church on Sunday. My mother never cajoled us into going. My father said, "This bus leaves at nine. Make sure you are in the car when it's time to go."

Yet I see mothers and fathers today who come to me for prayer for their children. I ask where the children are so I can pray for them. They tell me, "I couldn't make them come. I couldn't force them to come to church because I didn't want them to be mad at me. I don't want them to wind up hating church!"

I then ask, "What do you do on Monday when it's time for them to go to school?"

They stare at me as though I'm from Mars and reply, "Well, of course, they *have to go to school.* It's the law."

My heart breaks because I realize these parents unwittingly have built a sheepfold for their children on the east side of Jordan. Those same mothers will be in the prayer line asking prayer for their children because they don't know what to do with them when they have become rebellious. Your child is going to be mad anyway. *Let him be mad in church.*

Feel Like Compromising? Don't!

THE SECOND thing the Lord told me would keep us from possessing His best is *compromise.*

Remember, Reuben and Gad told Moses they would go across the Jordan but would *leave their children behind* on the east side. I have asked parents during special conferences and weekday services where their children are. "Oh, they go to a Christian school, and they have too much homework."

My father and mother never permitted us to bring all of our homework and spread it all over the church floor along with little matchbox cars and coloring books. Those were the days before children's church. Thank God, we now have services especially designed for our youth. My parents' attitude was, "We're going across—*and you're coming with us.*"

My mother sat us on either side of her, and if we didn't listen, she would slip her hand under the fat part of our thighs where no one could see and twist until it brought tears to our eyes. We *were* going to sit still in church. (I wonder if it's too late to report her to the child-abuse authorities!)

Those were the days when you didn't put the special speaker in a hotel. I think back then there were only about five hotels in the whole United States, and they were all Howard Johnsons! The evangelist would stay at the pastor's house. And because I was the only daughter, he would be given my room.

Never once did my mother say, "Oh, Cathy, honey—I hope this doesn't give you a dysfunctional dysfunction and cause you years of therapy and inner healing and deliverance—but we need to use your room."

No. My mother said to me, "When you get home from school, change the sheets. The evangelist is staying here. He will be sleeping in your bed. You'll sleep on the couch." It did not give me a dysfunction, but it did teach sacrifice and honoring the gift of God. My parents' testimony to this day is that their children and their children's children walk with God. We have spouses who walk with God. Even our pets walk with God. (I'm sure I saw my poodle slain in the Spirit last night.)

Don't compromise. Don't build a sheepfold on the east side for your children so they can lag behind.

Too Busy? So Am I!

THE THIRD thing the Holy Spirit told me would keep us from having the best is *busyness*. We are just too busy.

We have never been so busy, doing so many good things. I know what busy is. Believe me, I do understand. As parents, we make sure our children don't miss soccer practice,

Boy Scout meetings, Campfire Girls, Woodchuck Boys, karate class, ballet, and snot-blowing etiquette school. Yet the things of the Spirit of God are much more important. All those other things are not wrong. They're not sin. They just cannot be our number-one priority.

I desire the very best for my children. I know you do too. I have never heard a pregnant woman say, "You know, I don't expect much from my child. As long as he has nine out of ten toes and has an IQ a few points above a moron, it doesn't matter."

No! I want my son to be a Heisman trophy winner. I want my daughter to be the star of the school play. I want my children to serve in the house of God. I want them to have the very best.

That's how God feels about you and me. That's why the Lord took the children out of Egypt to the Promised Land. He wanted them to have the very best.

What happened to Reuben and Gad? They lost their land.

Have you ever been to Israel? The east side of Jordan is nothing more than desert, and it only serves the nomad. On the west side of Jordan the lush landscape produces fruits, flowers, and vegetables, and it has been established to God's people as an inheritance forever. So it is today.

The east side is the easy side to camp on, but it is not where you belong. The west side might be a little harder to cultivate, but it's where the milk and honey flow.

What will it be—the east side or the west side? The possible or the impossible? Which side of Jordan is for you?

Rise up, O saints of God; it's worth it! Arm yourself. Let's go.

Five

HEY! SOMEONE FORGOT TO TELL ME ABOUT THE WILDERNESS!

I WAS frantically searching through my nightstand drawer for a scrap of paper and a pen to write down the toll-free number for the new Thunder Thigh, butt-shrinking, belly-flattening exercise machine. I just had to have it. It looked so easy. The two-hour informercial convinced me that for just four payments of $39.95 plus $299.95 postage and handling I could actually look like the woman demonstrating this glorious piece of machinery. Of course, she was a foot taller than me, never broke a sweat, and never did more than five repetitions at once—which should have been a clue.

I'm a sucker for these informercials. I think the people who write them sit in a room with my picture before them, thinking stuff up and shrieking hysterically as they come up with the *next* useless item they plan to sell me.

It arrived in a box that no one could lift. My children love the Thunder Thigh. They hang upside down from the bars and try to grind each other up when one falls under the foot pedal. As a side benefit, my husband also enjoys the machine. He hangs his sweaty suit coat over it after he has finished preaching.

One day the Thunder Thigh was an absolute lifesaver for me... a godsend. When I needed some batteries for my Walkman, I remembered that I had installed two into that piece of equipment. Presto! I had my answer.

I still have the Thunder Thigh. But I do not look like the lady on television. Sadly, I have finally resigned myself to the fact that I will never be chosen for the *Sports Illustrated* swimsuit cover even if I *were* taller. However, there is still something in me that drives me on past my skepticism for finding the latest shortcut to a great body.

I am writing this while staring at the Thunder Thigh equipment and eating Raisinets.

POWER TO CHANGE

I WAS so glad when God began to release revelation on the word of faith and the power of God's Word in our mouth— the power of a positive confession, the ability to change things in the Spirit, and to bring to pass promises with aggressive spiritual warfare. What I did not hear, if indeed it was told to me, is that after the promise there is a season of waiting that we will walk through if we are to have God's very best.

Last year the Lord dropped a seed of faith into my heart to believe Him for a larger home. Randi and I were living in a lovely home that we were buying but had not yet closed on. With our six children, it was too small. When we tried to expand the house, the builders informed us that the foundation would not endure another level and the covenant community bylaws would not allow us to build onto the back of the house. I think that was due to the fact that it would block one of the neighbor's views of the half-dead squirrel on top of a half-dead oak tree.

Through this great revelation that God gave me—the revelation that since I had more children than I had room for we needed a larger home—God dropped the desire and the faith into my heart to begin to look for a larger home.

I started looking through the newspaper, and what I found was that we could not even come close to buying what we needed. The one ad I responded to didn't say much about the house. The owners said, "You really have to see it in order to appreciate it!" I should have known....

We pulled into a neighborhood where, quite frankly, I didn't believe we could even afford the rent on the gatehouse. Following the directions, we drove up to a lovely home. A lady answered our knock and invited us in. My mouth literally dropped open. It was the most beautiful and spacious home I had ever seen.

As she began showing us through the house, I knew she didn't have to sell me. I was convinced. However, my husband had forewarned me all the way there: "Don't say anything! Don't talk. Keep your mouth shut!" He knows I am not the negotiator in the family. I would sign everything in a heartbeat, just as I did for the fat-burning Abflex Roller.

The owner took us into the living room and dining room, just like the one where I had always envisioned my children sitting around the table in little Laura Ashley and Ralph Lauren outfits. We went through the family room, then into the bedrooms.

She said, "I don't know if you have little boys, but this bedroom has already been decorated for boys." It was done in a sports motif, perfect for a boy's bedroom. It even had its own bathroom.

Then we moved into the adorable room already decorated for a little girl, baby dolls on the wallpaper and all. It had a separate bathroom (with a separate bidet that my boys love to use for a drinking fountain—and if you don't know what a bidet is, then you haven't made that paradigm shift yet.)

Upstairs the owner showed us a room she had made into

a bonus room, or playroom, for the children, with its own attached bedroom and bath, just in case. Of course, it was perfect for us because our secretary lives with us!

By this time tears were rolling down my cheeks. Randi said to me, "Now, honey, just because it appears by all circumstances that it is God's will for us to buy this house, it doesn't automatically mean it is!"

I said, "I understand the principle of what you are saying, but couldn't it just this *one time* be God's will?"

"The House Costs How Much?"

AFTER WE saw the house, we asked the selling price. When the owner told us, my heart sank—the amount was so far beyond what I could believe God for—I did not have the faith for it. I began to wish we hadn't even gone to see it.

But the promise has the ability to do that to you. You see, God issues a challenge for you to *do something very difficult*. That's the first step in God's process to bring you into His best. That thing that He has challenged you to believe Him for is much larger than you. In fact, it's bigger than you can comprehend. You will hear this theme over and over in this book: If your promise isn't big enough to frighten you, then it's not God. What God gives us is always bigger, but so is the faith challenge that precedes it.

Immediately the challenge God gives us invokes fear. Why? Because there is negative and positive stuff going on inside us. Our hearts begin to war within us. What happens is that the Lord gives us promises concerning the challenge. He may send a prophet to prophesy, or He may give us a scripture verse to hang on to. Our hearts will leap within us, and we will have a greater vision.

As I was walking out of that beautiful house that day, the Spirit of the Lord spoke to me and said, "If you want that house, I'll give it to you." I shared this with my husband, and we prayed and agreed together that if it was really God, and if we had really heard from Him, He would give us this house.

CHOOSE NOW THIS DAY ...

THE NEXT step in God's process to bring you into His best is simply this: *Make a choice.* You have heard the challenge of the Lord and have seen what things look like in the natural realm, and now you must choose.

Will you believe God or doubt Him? Enter into faith or remain locked in fear? Obey or disobey Him? The choice is simple—keep things just the way they are and have what you have always had, or step out by faith and have what you've never had but always desired and dreamed of possessing.

We chose. Randi and I stepped out in faith and told the owner of the home we were living in at the time that we were going to move. At the same time Randi began negotiations to purchase the new house.

Beloved reader, I want to give you a principle that I missed somewhere along the way. I always thought that if you believed God, prayed, sowed some seed, and made the proper confession—BAM! You had whatever you confessed. I would like to find the person who taught me that, ring their doorbell, and run!

You see, to make the right choice immediately brings you into the third step of God's plan for the best: *CRISIS!*

No, this is not a typo. And no, I'm not making a negative confession. Weathering crisis is a principle in God. The choices we make to do right and have God's best will, for a short season, lead us through crisis. Allow me to illustrate.

When we told the owner of the house we were living in that we planned to move, he responded by telling us, in the nicest manner, that he would probably sue us. No amount of reasoning would move him. We appealed to him on the basis that the house was too small for our family and that it could not be expanded. To expand the house was part of our original agreement. *Too bad,* was his sentiment. To top it all, we were informed that we would be responsible for the house payments for the remainder of the lease or until the owner sold it to someone else.

Knowing that moving was now a reality, we kept pressing forward. Negotiations had been going great for the new house—that is, until we hit a snag. The conversation went something like this:

HOMEOWNERS: We need a check for seventy zillion dollars as a down payment.

RANDI (HESITANTLY): Okay. How about *nothing* down?

HOMEOWNERS: All right, then sixty-five zillion dollars down.

RANDI: Ummmm. Let's say *nothing!*

This went on for a month until the owners realized we really didn't have that kind of money to buy a house, so they put the house back on the market.

Meanwhile, the house we were living in was in the process of being put back on the market, and the owner told us, in the nicest possible way of course, that he wanted us OUT!

Talk about a crisis! The first part of crisis is that your choice is now pulling you apart. You have an established way of doing things, and you are not comfortable doing it any other way. Now you are being required to change.

The second part of the crisis comes because we do not live all alone on an island; therefore, when we begin to make choices that affect those around us, our crisis also becomes a crisis for everyone else. We, on the other hand, have moved from crisis to *chaos.*

Very loudly I had told everyone that God was going to give us this beautiful new home by performing a miracle, blah, blah, blah. Now here I was, sitting in the middle of a home that was too small, that was now filled to the sides with all of our boxes, with an irate landlord bearing down on us, pressuring us to move—and nowhere to go.

How many times do we pull away from making tough choices because we can see the crisis that choice will bring? Many cry out, "Oh, no, not another problem! My plate is too full already." Then they say *no* to the very thing that God wants to use to take them out of the cycle of hopelessness and into the promise.

A "Grace-and-Favor" Home

IN THE midst of all this, my *Majesty* magazine arrived in the mail. No, it is not a publication from Bill and Gloria Gaither; it is from the United Kingdom. It is an update on the royal family. I subscribe to it in the unlikely event that I am ever called on to prophesy to, say… Queen Elizabeth.

The magazine featured an article about an Australian who was hired by Buckingham Palace as part of its press pool. He had so distinguished himself among his peers that when the palace announced the separation of the Duke and Duchess of Windsor the queen immediately assigned the Australian as Sarah Ferguson's press representative. Because he had handled himself honorably in representing the queen, she gave him a second promotion.

When the palace announced the separation of Prince Charles and the late Princess of Wales, the queen placed this Australian as head of Diana's press corps. After Diana gave her authorized interview to the BBC, the press representative immediately resigned out of respect for his queen.

This is where the article got really exciting in my opinion. When Queen Elizabeth saw his loyalty to her, she immediately promoted him to the head of all the press corps at Buckingham Palace. The author wrote, "The Aussie is a very devout born-again Christian." He further stated that as a part of his promotion the queen had granted him a "grace-and-favor" home in St. James Palace.

When I finished reading the article, the Holy Spirit immediately spoke to me and said, "Cathy, because of Randi's and your devotion and loyalty to the Sovereign, I am giving *you* a 'grace-and-favor' home."

It was suddenly so clear! The Australian had received a home he couldn't afford, in a neighborhood he couldn't afford, as a part of the favor and grace of his sovereign. The Lord was now giving us a home we couldn't afford, in a neighborhood we couldn't afford, as part of His favor and grace!

That day I knew it. The next day I had to leave for Bangor, Maine, for a conference. Also, it was the day my husband felt he should go once more to negotiate for the new house. Before I left, we agreed together that God would work for us. We decided that we were not going to lose our victory, joy, or testimony for something as temporary as a building. However, if this was the blessing God had for us, then we would press in until we received an answer.

"We're Moving!"

SITTING IN Pastor Ron Durham's office after an awesome service in Bangor, he jokingly asked me what I would be doing the next week. "I'm moving, Pastor Ron."

"Oh, really? Where?"

"I don't know yet."

I told him the whole story, knowing that he and his wife, Lynne, would understand and be in prayer with us. Then he asked me if I was upset and afraid. My answer was, "No, because I've been at this spiritual point before."

There is one thing that crisis and chaos have taught us. That is, *God always has a plan!* We may not be able to see it because it is higher than our plan. It may be obscured, may be better, may be in a different city or another church, but God is God, and we are not!

Randi called me that night and was jubilant. He had met once more with the owners. They had discussed the situation and had decided to take whatever down payment we would offer. Then they gave him the key to the house!

We moved in the next day. The house we had been living in sold almost immediately, short-circuiting a lawsuit and a long, drawn-out ordeal. AWESOME!

The mind is the first battleground. How do you keep from losing it in the middle of the battle? There are two secrets that will help us come into the presence of God.

LET ME SHARE TWO SECRETS ...

FIRST, *STAY in communion with the Lord*. The temptation during crisis is to focus on the problem, the people, and a solution. Our flesh wants to *do* something—anything—to bring about the quickest possible solution. Many times God's way is not the most expedient way. As we stay in communion and fellowship with our God, He will keep us in perfect peace.

The other secret is *to communicate*. Of course, when I'm going through a crisis, my tendency is to clam up and pull away because I don't want to *bother* anyone with my problems. NOT! Truthfully, my tendency is to yell loudly, call every prayer tower and television ministry on the face of the earth, and annoy my friends with my problems to the point of being obnoxious. I have long suspected that caller ID was invented because of my being in crisis.

There are times when I have had to grab my pastor by the lapels and tell him, "Pray for me, hang on to me! I'm going through a hard time, and I need you—I need the body of Christ—to pray for me, feed me chocolate, pat my head, and tell me everything is going to be all right."

Communicate with your family, even with unsaved loved ones. Here is an example of a conversation you may use with your loved one when you are experiencing crisis.

YOU (HELGA): Oh, God, Oh, God. Help.

YOUR LOVED ONE (SNODBERT): What in the world is wrong with you, Helga?

YOU (HELGA): I don't know. Hormones, PMS, short-term memory loss, your mother. Oh, God, help.

YOUR LOVED ONE (SNODBERT): Helga, you're sitting on the channel-changer. Move.

Okay—just kidding. Don't try that. That conversation was

just an example of two people who do not know how to communicate. Either that, or they have a really bad marriage.

But communicate anyway! When you are facing a crisis, the Holy Spirit will give you the words to share your heartfelt needs with even the hardest of hearts. If you will hold fast, such communication will bring forth the kind of change that glorifies God. But most importantly, don't just look for change in your house, your family, ministry, or finances. Look for change within *yourself.*

You are a grace-and-favor miracle!

Six

ARE YOU LIVING IN A TENT OR A PALACE?

FOR every great man or woman of God who achieves anything by the Spirit of God, such achievement is usually preceded by a crisis time that comes into their lives to propel them to the forefront.

I am so glad there were men and women of God who went before us and stood for things that were at first rejected by the body of Christ. I have a classic Pentecostal background. Then I married this crazy Jewish fellow, and he began talking to me about Derek Prince and deliverance. I told him that what Derek Prince was teaching was not true... because *we didn't teach that* in our denomination when I was growing up.

Derek Prince took a lot of flak from the body of Christ and was even considered by some as a heretic, until a few of us decided we didn't want to live with our demons anymore and began to buy his books.

Next came along a man named Kenneth Hagin, preaching and teaching on the topics of faith and prosperity. Christians got their pantyhose in a knot and got all upset. "He's a heretic; it's a get-rich-quick scheme." Aren't you glad Kenneth Hagin didn't pay any attention to us but kept right on teaching and stepping out—preaching the word of faith? Eventually, when we became sick enough of being poor and not having anything and tired enough of not being able to pay our bills, we became a bit more receptive. And when someone gave us a tape or a book by Brother Hagin, a light went on in our heads and we said, "*I believe God;* He wants me to prosper."

To everyone who makes their mark in the kingdom of God there comes a season when they have to step out of the crowd. It usually takes a crisis for a person to actually do this because no one really wants to do that willingly. It takes crisis to propel a person to the forefront of ministry.

The Propellant of Crisis

How God is able to use you in the days to come largely depends on how you deal with crisis in your life. I can look back on the seasons of my life and say, "Here was a place when I was tempted to run, give up, go back, let go, and quit."

Using 20/20 hindsight, I can look back on my life and see crossroads. And if you're anything like me, you can always see better when you are on the other side of things. One of the crossroads of my life was when the Spirit of the Lord gave me an opportunity to choose how I was going to walk with Him.

I am sharing from my heart. I am aware that there are some traditional mindsets that may diametrically oppose what I am saying. If you don't agree with me, it's all right; *just don't tell me.* I don't want a spirit of rejection! However, please think about what I am saying to you.

I want to give you a charge. I want to talk to you about the difference between *purpose* and *permission.*

PERFECT VS. PERMISSIVE

WE'VE ALL heard that there is a perfect will of God and a permissive will of God. Then someone else said there is no permissive will of God; either you *are in* His perfect will, or you *are not*.

The Lord has been dealing with me concerning this. I feel that if He is dealing with me, why shouldn't He deal with you as well? I am not talking about the difference between the permissive will of God and the perfect will of God, but rather the difference between the PURPOSE of God and His permissive will. Am I going to live in His purpose or reside in His permission?

There are many today who are living in His *permission,* but they are not living in His *purpose.* The Word tells us that only about one-fourth of all believers will live in the pure purpose of God—and the rest are simply too tired to do it.

So there comes a time when you must decide that this is just the way it is. You must get used to being tired. You must press through anyway, tired or not. There are many who will miss the purpose of God because they became *tired* and started to coast. Many believers don't get up and go to church on Sunday morning because they are *tired.* They won't miss heaven, but they may have missed His purpose.

WHERE ARE YOU?

AM I in His purpose, or am I in His permission? This may sound like just the opposite of what I have been saying about crossing the line, stretching out, taking a risk, and obeying God. It may seem as if I am contradicting myself. However, it's called *the other side of the coin,* or the balance. I'd rather be doing *something* for God than *nothing.* If I'm going to be guilty, I'd rather be guilty of mercy than judgment, of over-giving than of being stingy, of giving something away because I was emotionally moved than of worrying that my husband would be mad at me for giving so hilariously. I always say, "It is much easier to ask forgiveness than permission!"

The devil is in the permissive will of God. He can't do anything without God's permission. Some people think the devil is like Darth Vader and that God is like Luke Skywalker from the movie, *Star Wars*. They think there is a continual struggle for good and evil and that eventually God wins.

You know that the devil was created by God. The Creator is *always* greater than His creation. Too much glory and credit are given to the devil. Sometimes it's just life.

I have heard Christians say, "I bind that spirit that made McDonald's run out of Egg McMuffins!" Oh, give me a break! Sometimes they just run out of Egg McMuffins! It's not the devil. It's just life!

The devil is operating in the permissive will of God. Samuel clearly revealed that God did not want the people of Israel to have a king. God said, "I want to be your King." But the Israelites wanted to be like everyone else. So He permitted them to have a king. That king was Saul. He eventually turned to the occult and became a madman. We know from the examples of King Saul and others that there will never be peace on earth until Jesus is crowned King.

If you live in a place where Jesus is not your King, you are living where you do not have peace. If you are reading this book and you do not have peace, perhaps you are living in God's permissive will. You are always crying because you feel the devil is constantly on your case and everything is going bad for you. If that is so, it may be because Jesus is not your King. Are you walking around in permission instead of purpose?

Have we, like the children of Israel, grown insensitive to God's *purpose* because we've been residing in His *permission* for so long? Have we been choosing on our own without first praying? Have we been making our own agendas without first consulting Him?

I love to press on. I'm the first one to cross the line. Just show me where to sign up! I believe women are ready to run because they've been to the gynecologist and no longer have any pride or image. When you've been to the OB/GYN, laying face-up in a paper dress on a cold examination table while trying to make conversation as you examine the holes in the ceiling, you lose a certain amount of pride and image.

When you're laying flat on your back, it really gives the Lord a wonderful opportunity to speak to you, doesn't it? So it has been in my case.

Now I'll admit it: I'm the first one to give, the first one to do what is asked. However, there are times in my life when God has said, "Slow down; I want to talk to you. I need to speak to you about some things."

LET'S NOT BE DECEIVED

HAVE WE been in permission for so long that we mistake it for the perfect purpose of God for our lives? We live far below His purpose. Have we demanded our way for so long that He has given us what we demanded? Have we then mistaken His giving of those things that we have for permission for His loving purpose, so that we have made it to be our way of life? We deceive ourselves, believing we are in His perfect will because we have lived that way for so long. But we are living in permission, not purpose.

I want to repeat: *Have we demanded our way for so long that He has given us what we demanded? Have we then mistaken His giving of those things as His loving purpose so that we made it our way of life? Are we deceiving ourselves into believing that we are in His perfect will?*

I want to share a story with you, taking the risk that you will despise me—*despise* meaning "to think little of me." I have gotten to the point where I don't have any agenda, and I humbly pray that I don't have any ambition. My heart is really to be at home with my children. Anyone who knows me knows that I enjoy being a mother and a wife. But I also love to minister and see God's people set free. So if you think less of me for admitting to being pulled in two directions, there is nothing I can do about it.

I have shared with you that I wanted more children and that I did everything I knew in order to conceive. I tried to twist God's arm by reminding Him of all the Hollywood stars who are having babies out of wedlock and of the scores of people who don't want to be pregnant who are getting pregnant anyway. I told Him I just didn't understand it. I did it all. I rubbed baby booties on my belly. I hung prayer cloths on the bed post. I took enough fertility medicine to have a litter, and I even put my husband in boxer shorts—which he didn't like—to increase his sperm count. (That's what I was told would result, anyway!)

God's Way of Getting Through

WHEN JERUSHA was about eight years old, someone called me and told me of a girl who was pregnant and who was going to give up the child. She said if I wanted the baby, she could arrange a meeting with the mother. Of course, I immediately agreed. Something inside of me, my "knower," said, "Don't do this!" However, I wanted a baby so badly about then I would have done anything.

My "knower" kept warning me, "Cathy!" I didn't tell anyone, but I just kept pushing past my "knower," past the peace of God. The Word tells us that we don't have to have a specific prophetic word. We must let our hearts and minds be ruled by the peace of God. I pushed past peace because I *wanted* that baby!

I was on my way to meet this girl when someone walked in front of my Toyota, causing me to swerve to avoid hitting him. I couldn't remember whether or not I was to steer into the slide. Someone reminded me later that advice was for ice and that I was in Florida.

I skidded sideways, and by a miracle of God there was no car in my path as I skidded across the road into a ravine, hitting a telephone pole. Instinctively I put my arm up to protect my face as I slid to the passenger side of the car and was pulled back by my seatbelt.

I was semiconscious as an ambulance rushed me to the hospital, and I was praying in the Spirit. I asked the emergency people to take me to the church because I knew that if I could just get to my husband he would pray for me. The emergency technicians ignored my request and rushed me to the hospital, calling ahead with all the initial information about my injuries.

My husband rushed to the hospital, burst through the emergency room doors as only he can do, and upon seeing me cried, "Oh, my poor baby! Look what the devil did to you!" I thought, *That's right; it was the devil, not my bad driving*. I was hoping Randi would remember that later when the hospital bill came in the mail.

The doctor sent for my family because of the seriousness of my injuries. He told my mother that I couldn't focus because my brain was swelling; that's why everything was fuzzy to me. My dear mother simply replied, "Oh, she's always like that."

They took several sets of x-rays before the neurosurgeon was sent in to begin surgery. My husband prayed for me before he would let me go into surgery. They kept taking more x-rays and finally had to admit that *something* had happened to me since they brought me in. The final x-ray showed there were no broken bones in my body. But as a souvenir, I have the scars from sixty-four stitches in my arm where they removed the glass.

When the state trooper came to talk to me, I explained that if that stupid telephone pole hadn't been in the way I would have only suffered embarrassment.

The trooper said, "Mrs. Lechner, you don't understand. If you had *not* hit that telephone pole your car would have flipped upside down, and you would have been crushed or drowned before we could have reached you. Hitting that telephone pole righted the car and saved your life."

I said, "Thank you, telephone pole; bless you!"

Seen Any Telephone Poles Lately?

SOME OF you have telephone poles in your life that you have been cursing. God, in His infinite mercy and grace, let you hit a telephone pole in order to save your life. You were cursing hitting the pole, when the enemy had something far worse planned for you just down the road.

Randi and I later learned that woman I was going to meet was a heavy drug user. The baby was born with severe deformities that we would have been totally responsible for financially. The child died six weeks later.

I had moved out of my "knower" into demanding my way because I knew what God wanted to do. I knew He had more children for us, but I was eight years ahead of His purpose.

I can't tell you to push forward and press ahead without also telling you, "Don't violate the peace of God that's on the inside of you." He gave you that peace for a purpose. The Word tells us that He causes all things to "work together for good to them . . . who are the called according to his purpose" (Rom. 8:28). *He has a purpose.*

Things *will not* work together for good if you are not in His purpose but are simply in His permission.

Do we walk with Him according to *His* purpose, or do we walk according to *our* purpose? Do we have our good purposes in mind, or do we have His "God" purposes in mind? Do we forsake our lives to serve Him and His purposes, or do we twist His Word to make it *appear* that He came to serve us and bring our dreams to pass? Did He really come to make us His brethren and sons of His Father so that through us He might have *His* dreams fulfilled in the earth, or are we just caught up in making *our* dreams come to pass?

If you know me at all, you know I am a dream-giver. I want

to lift you and encourage you to move into the will of God.

But I will also be the first one to tell you that we cannot forget that God gave of Himself so He could bring about His glory and His purpose in the earth. While He's at it, *we get the blessing.*

When we stand before Him, will we hear, "Well?" or will we hear, "Well done"? I don't want just a touch of the Holy Spirit; I want His purpose fulfilled in my life. I want Him to change those things about my life that need to be changed in order for His purpose to be fulfilled.

GOD TRIES OUR MOTIVES

WHAT YOU do is your wood, hay, and stubble. *Why you do it* is your gold. You can judge a man's *what,* but you are forbidden to judge his *why.*

A man whom I greatly admire moves in the prophetic like no one I have ever seen. He can tell you what you ate for lunch if it is important for him to know it and for you to hear it. (Of course, *you* know what you had for lunch; you ordered it from the menu!) He had a tremendous impact on me and upon all those around him. Suddenly, he was nowhere around. God seemed to absolutely take him out of circulation and set him on a shelf. It was as if his entire ministry dried up. I asked God, "Why?"

He said, "Because his gifting exceeds his character. Because his character could not keep up with his gifting he would have lost the race."

God is more interested in your character than He is in your gifting because your gifting will pass away. What does it profit a man if he prophesies to millions and loses his own soul?

The Lord spoke to me early one morning and said, "The purpose of My heart in this hour is to bring men and women of God together to break down dividing walls so they can see where nobody's name could be put to it." It's a God-thing; it's not a man-thing.

"Lord, Send Them!"

IN THE early part of this year I was crying out to the Lord. I hadn't unpacked from the last trip. I was in my prayer time. I said, "Lord, I don't want to go anymore! There are a million holy ladies out there, all saying, 'Send me, send me!'

"Lord, send them. I miss my husband. I miss my kids. I want to stay home. Lord, please, I'm tired, and I don't want to go anymore."

I heard the Holy Spirit speak, and He sounded just like my dad when he speaks to me. He said, "Cathy, love your husband, love your children, but *serve* your God. There's purpose for you, and you've got to walk in it."

I am to *love* you, but I'm not to *live* according to you. I am to live according to God's purposes. Don't misunderstand me; I am not recommending anarchy and not being submissive to pastors and teachers. I am not advocating women not being submissive to their husbands. But I want to tell you, wives, the day is coming when you will stand and give an account to God for what He has put into your hands. On that day you will not be able to say, "Well, my husband..."

I have also seen women use submission as an excuse not to obey God. "I felt led to stay home and be with my husband." This means he was sitting there watching the ballgame and you were doing laundry. One of you might as well go to church and be happy. "Well, he just won't let me give." Honey, you buy whatever you want to buy. I know women. They'll charge it or do whatever they have to do to get what they want. So if you want to give badly enough, you'll find a way to do it.

I want to live according to God's purpose in my life. There was a time when God asked me to do something. I said to my husband, "Honey, I feel as if the Lord asked me to do this."

Randi said *no.*

I said okay.

I came back to Randi later and told him that God would not release me from this thing, and again he said *no*.

I told him okay. But God would not release me, and I tried to argue with Him that Randi would probably just say no again.

The Lord said, "Go again."

So I went back to Randi and said, "God will not release me. You've got to go and ask the Lord. Don't make me choose between you and my God—I loved Him before I loved you."

He responded, "Go obey God."

STAY IN THE PERFECT WILL OF GOD

WHENEVER YOU are offended you will be pushed out of God's purpose into His permission.

What about the story of Paul and Barnabas? Saul (later known as the apostle Paul) was killing Christians. Barnabas was preaching the gospel. All of a sudden Saul had his Damascus Road conversion, was dramatically saved, and God put him under submission to Barnabas.

> Now in the church (assembly) at Antioch there were prophets—inspired interpreters of the will and purposes of God—and teachers, Barnabas, Symeon who was called Niger [black], Lucius of Cyrene, Manaen a member of the court of Herod the tetrarch, and Saul.
>
> —ACTS 13:1, AMP

God had put Saul under Barnabas to be discipled, mentored, and taught. While the two were fasting and worshiping the Lord, the Holy Spirit said, "Separate now for me Barnabas and Saul." In the Word the most important one was always named first. Barnabas was the teacher. So in this case his name was mentioned first, in respect for his stature in the Lord. Later on the two were referred to as Paul and Barnabas. Even later, contention developed between them, and they began to fight over one of the disciples—John Mark. That contention forced Paul and Barnabas out of the purpose of God, which was for them to minister together. It separated them into permission.

What I am trying to tell you is that contention always causes us to think, *I'm right; you're wrong.* Contention and offenses will cause us to separate ourselves from some of those with whom God has purposed for us to walk. Because He loves us and He sees that we cannot walk together, many times He allows us to go our separate ways, and we walk on in His permission.

There are many who are right now wandering around in permission. Many have truth in them, but they themselves are not truth. A man of truth who himself is also true to the Lord *is truth*.

God brings us to a place where we will have peace, no matter what. If God in His wisdom permits what He could have prevented in His power, then you can trust that it's for a purpose. It's so that you will bow at His throne and say, "So be it, Lord, amen. I trust You. I live according to Your purpose."

I know that the will of God is not always pleasant. Sometimes it is difficult and rubs us the wrong way. We do not like it. We confessed it another way. The word we got does not live up with what is happening. What God told us and what is happening seem to be in conflict. But when God does it, you say, "God, You could have stopped this from happening. Why didn't You?"

It's so we will bow at His throne and say, "God, I thank You and praise You. I believe that You are working all things for my good because I am not living in Your permission; I am living in Your purpose. Don't let me live in Your permission. Let me live only in Your purpose. If what I am going through serves Your purpose, then let it be so, Lord. Amen!"

After the incident with the baby I said, "God, You've given me a promise. I'm going to stand; I'm going to declare it. I don't understand why You have not done this for me. I serve You. I love You. I give. I've done everything I know to do. There is not one reason that the doctor can give me or that You can give me as to why You have not moved on my behalf concerning this. I am taking a step back and trusting You."

God Moves—Perfectly!

EIGHT YEARS later as I was walking along in His purpose, BOOM! BOOM! BOOM! BOOM! BOOM! BOOM! Six times God moved—each time perfectly.

I want to encourage all you singles: Don't live in God's permission. Don't get in bed with His permission. Wait for His purpose.

My secretary has been with me for almost thirteen years. She's thirty-six years old and has never been married. She is believing God to bring her a husband. I met her in Seattle, Washington. She sold everything she owned and moved to Florida, just to serve me. I said to her, "God had to look all over the world to find someone who could help me raise these babies for Him. Little did you know thirteen years ago that God was setting you up for the great destiny that He has for you." I told her that He had a man of God for her and that the longer she waits, the better he gets.

Some say, "It is easier for me to get hit by a sniper on assignment for Yasir Arafat than it will be for me to be married by the time my body parts go south." I pooh-pooh that statement. If God can send a bunch of stinking camels out to find a wife for Isaac, He can surely find a mate for you. However, you must wait for His purpose.

I am touching some sacred cows, I know—but please forgive me. If you don't agree with me, it's all right. I don't mind. Just don't tell me.

"How Long, Lord?"

I LOVE to bind, loose, and pray with the best of you. It

gives me a sense that I am accomplishing something in the Spirit. This is true especially if a spirit of heaviness comes over me. I could just bind and rebuke all day.

But how long is long enough? How long do we bind? Someone once gave me a book that said I was doing it all wrong. I was binding what I was supposed to be loosing and loosing what should have been bound. I got all confused. Have you ever seen people who get into intercession and frighten you? Have you ever had some of the holy ladies screw up their faces, point those bony fingers, and start rebuking you? That's scary!

The Lord has given us ownership of this earth. When we have dominion and ownership, there is a power and authority that is expressed. That's why Jesus was able to walk in and make the devils tremble. That's why Peter's shadow was so powerful.

I recently did a taping for a powerful ministry. I had never met the man who headed up this ministry, but when he entered the room it seemed as if he were nine feet tall. When he walked in I just knew I could hear everyone gulp. There was a *presence* about him when he entered the room. There was something about him that said he walked in authority.

When there is such power in authority that is expressed, you don't have to spend all day screaming your lungs out at the devil. You can do your warfare and then enter into praise and worship.

> We love You, Lord, and we're going to build a habitat
> and a throne for You. We love and praise You, Lord.
> Down the mountain the river flows and brings
> refreshing wherever it goes.

We can sing, and we can dance and worship the Lord, therefore ushering in the presence of God.

I have a chair in my bedroom. I walk into the room, head directly for my chair, start to sit, and never wonder: *Should I sit down? Is this chair going to hold me?* I have no question in my mind. The chair is mine. It belongs to me. When my children are in my chair and see me coming, I don't have to tell them to get out of my chair—they just move out. When my husband heads for *his* chair, the kids get out immediately. Why? Because it is his chair.

So it is with the authority God gave you. You have an ownership in the earth. You need to grasp that and move in that authority. Don't live in your last revelation. Your last revelation becomes a rag with which to clean your dipstick. Don't live in first gear. Get in neutral gear. Prepare for change. "God, You said that all things work together because I am walking in Your purpose and You have allowed this."

Anyone who flies knows that you have to live that way. Planes are late, canceled, and you miss connections. Just getting my children ready for church and having one of them lose a shoe on the way, or seeing one put his finger down his throat just to see what he ate for breakfast, makes me get to the place where I can say, "It's no big, hairy deal!"

Some of you are always fretting. We are walking in His purpose, in His will. Don't spend your life fretting. Just let all that stuff roll off you. Get in neutral gear. The ultimate con is the enemy taking all your attention, sucking the life and joy out of you over stuff that really doesn't matter. In the light of eternity, *who cares?*

Remember—God Is for You!

LIVE ACCORDING to His purpose in your life. God understands things you don't. He may have a hidden agenda for your life and your situation, and just because you don't understand it doesn't mean He isn't working for you. He is absolutely crazy about you!

I remember as a ten-year-old that I wanted a Barbie Dream House so badly. Each time we went to the department store I would beg my parents for it. I even saved my money to buy one. My dad would try to discourage me by telling me I didn't really want one because they were so flimsy that they wouldn't last.

What I didn't know was that my parents had put one on layaway for me for Christmas. But I wanted it *now!* In my child's mind I couldn't understand why they wouldn't let me have it. I told my parents, "You hate me. Everyone has a Barbie Dream House with an actual plastic sliding door except me." I threw myself across my bed in a heap, sobbing horribly.

My parents didn't hate me. They were working things together to bless me so that I could keep my money and they could spend theirs to give me something I wanted.

Some of you have said the same thing to God: "You don't love me or You would do this for me! You wouldn't make me wait. Not if You really loved me. Why?"

Are you in a valley, and it hurts? Things have not gone the way you thought they were going to go. You lined up all your prophecies and listened to them over and over. It didn't happen the way you planned. Want to know why? Because God has a better plan. When it comes to pass, you will say, "Thank You, God."

God is poised and ready to show off His glory. If you don't dangle for a little while, how is He ever going to show Himself to you? I don't like to dangle, but I found that in the dangling His purpose is done, His strength comes, and His glory is revealed.

I charge you to be filled with His purpose and stay there. Stay in His glory.

Seven

AND TO THINK I ALMOST MISSED IT!

WE ARE preparing to be the warriors of the new millennium. Zion is calling us to a higher place of praise. So say this with me: "I am a survivor. The devil tried to kill me, destroy me, take my joy, my hope, my vision, and my dream, but God brought me through. Therefore, I have the power to go and kick devil-butt!"

I believe God will anoint these words and will call you by His Spirit so that you will want to respond to the Spirit of God in this manner.

I was in a meeting with Peter Lord, who taught on prayer. I love to pray, but as he talked about prayer I slid further and further down in my seat. Before he was finished I was on my face crying out to God to strengthen my prayer life.

My desire for you is that before you finish reading this chapter you will totally surrender and say, "Zion is calling me, and I have to go to a higher place of praise. I'm going to stand on His mountain, magnify His name, and tell every nation that He reigns."

Luke 8:5 is the parable of the sower.

> A sower went out to sow his seed; and as he sowed, some fell by the way side; and it was trodden down, and the fowls of the air devoured it. And some fell upon a rock; and as soon as it was sprung up, it withered away, because it lacked moisture. And some fell among thorns; and the thorns sprang up with it, and choked it. And other fell on good ground, and sprang up, and bare fruit an hundredfold. And when he had said these things, he cried, He that hath ears to hear, let him hear.
>
> —Luke 8:5–8

Jesus said, "You who have ears to hear, hear." In other words, there are some who will read this and "hear" and somehow before they are through with the chapter will click off. Jesus will be saying something vitally important, and He will be calling. He is appealing to them to hear. What He is saying is vital—a matter of life and death in the Spirit. But some will hear, and some will not. The Bible says this is so.

When you travel a lot and move in certain circles, there is a tendency to attract those who come to tell you how wonderfully you presented the Word of the Lord. The problem with that is that I don't want to be deceived. The thing that impresses God is not what I do in public, but what I am in private when no one sees me.

COURAGE TO CROSS THE LINE

I HAVE been crying out to God that I don't want all my rewards in this life. While ministering at a conference I was trying to get some much-needed rest in my motel room. I began to weep. My mother asked me if anything was wrong. I told her, "I don't want to receive all my rewards on this earth so that when I get to heaven all I have is a crummy rhinestone Jesus pin. When He passes by there will be many wonderful people throwing crowns at His feet, and there I'll be, throwing this dumb rhinestone pin, picking it up and throwing it down again, and again, and again. I don't want to get all my rewards here on earth! I want some things saved for me. I want to do some secret things. I want to do some obediences. I want to cross some lines knowing that only God knew what it would cost for me to have the courage to cross them!"

Let me tell you how that attitude begins. It begins by possessing the promise. I am in a mode to see God's people possess promises. I want to see you not just get a word, because "hope deferred makes the heart sick" (Prov. 13:12, NIV). I've had people tell me, "Don't give me another word that I'm gonna get a man! I want to know his name and address! Don't tell me I am going to come into financial blessing! Give me a date!" The Word says that it's with faith, patience, and perseverance that we inherit the promises. So let's develop some of each and get moving!

I'd love to go to bed one night and wake up the next morning and be like Marilyn Hickey, color-coordinated and calm so that nothing upsets me, sitting in my chair looking lovely with all my colors in the right family. But I never seem to get it all together quite that easily. My saying is, *If it's on sale, it must be mine.*

I don't know that I have exactly ever seen an angel. I know a lot of people who are always having visions. I don't have many, and they aren't even in color. They are mostly in black-and-white. In one instance, however, I was sound asleep, and I was awakened by the word, "Redeemed!"

My eyes opened wide, and I could sense the presence of a ministering angel standing beside me who had been sent from the throne of God. He was sent to call me to get up and pray. I got out of bed because *he* called me.

"Why Can't I Minister in My Muumuu?"

ONE OF the things the Lord called me to do this year was to go to Australia. I am not a traveling kind of person. I am a homebody. I like to stay at home and order take-out food. I don't like to leave my house. I like to be home. I don't even like to go shopping. I like to get in my muumuu and do mail-order. In fact, if I could minister in my muumuu I'd be the happiest person in the world.

I received an invitation to go to Australia. When I accepted it, it seemed like a wonderful idea. How many of you have ever responded to a special altar call, going forward crying and saying, "I'm Yours, Lord. Take me—everything I am, everything I've got!"?

As the departure date for Australia inched closer and closer, the more excuses I could think of so I wouldn't have to go: It's not convenient at this time; I don't want to leave the children; my hair isn't doing well; it's too far away; I have to sit still for a long time; once I'm on that plane I can't get off if I change my mind. You know the kinds of excuses I was coming up with—all of them lame.

I've been to many countries, including Japan, the Philippines, and Russia, but I'd rather stay in Jacksonville. Nevertheless, I decided I would go to Australia if God would give me peace about going. It wasn't my peace that was unsettled; it was my flesh.

I tried to make a deal with the Lord. I said that if they would send me a business-class plane ticket I would know that He definitely wanted me to go to Australia. It wasn't five minutes later that the telephone rang. The person on the other end said that although it was four o'clock in the morning there, she woke up and felt impressed to call and tell me that she was going to send me a business-class ticket to Australia.

I expressed my appreciation while inside I was groaning. Finally I told the Lord I would go and would even shut up and quit complaining; this was His will, and it was good. I could just hear the Holy Spirit saying, "Well, thank you. I appreciate that."

The whole time I was preparing to make this trip my flesh was giving me all sorts of problems. I walked through the airport crying, "For the glory of God and the building of the kingdom. For the glory of God and the building of the kingdom."

We were flying through the air, and, having nothing to do to occupy myself, I got out my praise-and-worship tapes and began to worship the Lord. As I did this, He spoke to me and said, "Cathy, that which you called uneasiness of your spirit wasn't a lack of peace; it was rebellion. You called it something spiritual, but you were behaving like Jonah. You just didn't want to go." When you are flying miles high in the sky with nothing but water far below you, it's very easy to repent; so I did—over and over again.

The first meeting we had was in the Australian capital of Canberra. The Lord gave me this word: "There's a witch in this place," I said. "I don't know anything about witchcraft, but I know there's a witch here and that you've come to put curses on this conference. There is a curse that has been sent out over your life, and within thirty days you will be dead if you do not come forward and publicly give your life to Christ. It isn't enough for you to do it in your seat. You must come up front."

At the end of the meeting a young woman came forward. Her shaved head was wrapped in a bandanna. She was heavily body-pierced and tattooed. In her hand she held bits of leather and paper that she was going to plant in the church.

She said, "I'm the witch. I've been sent by the coven in this city because we've heard that the prophets are here. I've been sent to put curses on every one of you. As you spoke, I knew it was me; I also know who has placed the curse against me." I told her we would pray and break that curse through the power and authority of the name of Jesus.

As we moved in to pray for this woman, she pulled back her fist to strike me. Now that's fine for other preachers, but I wasn't ready for that; I really didn't want to be hit. The Lord said, "Press in and put your arms around her; tell her that I love her." When I did that, she screamed and fell to the floor.

The Spirit of the Lord spoke to me and told me that she had never known the love of a man or woman. She had lived a lesbian lifestyle and had been abused by her mother and father. When I asked her to confirm that, she began to sob. That's why the Lord instructed me to put my arms around her: She had never known pure love from another woman. My ministry team and I put our arms around her, loved her, and prayed for her deliverance.

As I left the meeting that night, the Lord spoke to me and said, "And to think you almost missed it!"

PRAISE GOD—I DIDN'T MISS IT!

THE NEXT place we went to was a church in a small city outside Sydney. The leadership really didn't want me to minister. They already had a guest speaker scheduled. However, out of respect for Aussie prophet Steve Penny, the pastor reluctantly consented to let me speak in one service. He had never heard me and had no clue as to who I was.

As I stood to minister that morning, the Lord spoke to me about a young woman in the front row and said to tell her she was engaged to the wrong man. My heart and mind said, *I'd rather not. But, hey, I'm out of here after this morning; what can they do to me?*

So I obeyed the Lord and said, "Young lady, stand up. The Spirit of the Lord says you're engaged to the wrong man. If you will obey the Spirit of God and break this off, I will give you the man of God that I have prepared for you, and I will give him the woman of God." She didn't receive that word too well.

We were on our way to lunch after the service when the pastor asked me if I knew who the young woman was. I said I didn't. He said she was his daughter. *Oh, me!* I thought, *I must be going now. Just give me my skippy burger, and I will leave.*

He sat in his car and told me that for two years he and his wife had been trying to tell her that this man was not the one God had for her. "She won't listen to us. She has rebelled and moved out of the house. We have cried out to God and said, 'If it takes You sending a prophet to us to tell her it's not You, do whatever it takes, Lord, but spare our daughter.'"

As I sat in the backseat of that car the Spirit of God spoke to me and said, *"And you almost missed it because you didn't want to obey Me and sacrifice two weeks of your life."*

The pastor felt impressed that I should minister again that night. The evangelist who was supposed to be speaking was seated in the front row. I don't like to minister to ministers. It seems that everyone likes to do that. So I held back, but the Lord told me to prophesy the word of the Lord to him. In obedience, I asked him to stand. I said, "My brother, the Spirit of the Lord speaks to me and says this, 'I'm going to provide millions of dollars through the works of your hands.'" At this point his jaw fell open.

I continued, "I saw your works being put on tins and coffee mugs. You will be the next artist laureate of Australia. The finances will come in so that you can go and take a nation for Me."

This man cried out in a loud voice, "God!" and ran around the church.

When he came back to his seat I said, "The Spirit of the Lord further speaks, 'The Lord is giving you back your children. I've heard your desire for your six-bedroom house. It's on the way because your children are coming home!'"

He gave out with another, "God!" and took off running around the church again with everyone shouting and praising God.

After the service we were all in the pastor's ready room. The man I had prophesied to came in and said, "Do you know who I am? My name is Tim Hall. I am one of the premier evangelists in the country of Australia. I am also an artist. Here is a prototype cookie tin that we did to feature some of my work. Here is a coffee mug of some things that we are test-marketing. The current artist laureate of Australia is in his nineties, and he is not in good health. No one knew that it was my heart's cry to be the next artist laureate of this country."

He continued, "Years ago my wife left me while I was in ministry. My denomination kicked me out because I remarried. My former wife poisoned all my children against me. They all left, but I have been crying out to God to give me my children back. Two weeks ago one of my daughters called me and said that she was expecting a baby and wanted to come live with me. My son is coming to live with me. But we are in a two-bedroom apartment. I said, 'God, if this is You, we need a six-bedroom house.'"

He took me by the lapels of my jacket and said, "If you didn't come to Australia for anyone else, you came *for me!*"

I began to cry. When he asked me why I was crying, I said, *"Because I almost missed it."*

God Prepares the Way Anyway

WORD WAS traveling that God was sending His prophetic word to the country of Australia. All of a sudden I was in demand. But it wasn't due to anything in me; after all, I hadn't even wanted to go. I'm revealing my crummy side. It was God.

Next we went to a campground for a National Assemblies of God women's conference. They said the attendance had never been over sixty women. But this time the final attendance was four hundred because of the hunger of the women for the prophetic word.

I don't do campgrounds very well. My idea of camping is

slow room service. It wasn't very easy for me.

On the first night I was impressed to call for all the leadership to come forward. It was my intention to have them stand behind me and pray. The Lord said, "No, right now turn around and minister to the leaders." I usually start at the middle, but I felt the Lord say, "No. That end."

I said, "Daughter, I tell you that I have given a tithe of your city to you and the man of God. I tell you that God is in the house, and you will be world-renowned for the music that is in that place. But call the man of God and tell him that his vision is too small and his building is too small."

The place erupted, and she fell on her face before God. The next day she came to me and asked me if I knew who she was. Of course, I didn't. She told me her name and that she and her husband were prominent ministers in Australia. She asked, "Did you know?" I told her I didn't. She said, "I told my husband you didn't." She then testified to the accuracy of the word and the encouragement it brought and thanked me for my obedience.

When I got back to my room, I repented before the Lord. Do you know why? *Because I almost missed it!*

I want to tell you that there are things that the Spirit of God desires for you. There are things God wants you to do, and you are a split-second decision away from either walking into the will of God or shrinking back with fear.

Possessing the promise means, "I don't care, devil, how much you push. I don't care what you do. You are not pushing me off this mark. You are not going to make me crawl into a hole. I am not going to run away. I am not going to back down. My God has *promised!*"

Most of the time you say those words when *everything* is going wrong. How many of you know that life just stinks sometimes? Have you ever awakened and said, "Where's the abundant Christian life?" Be honest with me.

"Which Way Is Hell?"

IF YOU are going to win you must press toward the direction of hell. When I line up my life and compare it with what the Word of God says I'm supposed to have, what I'm supposed to be, and what I should be walking in, the reason I don't have these things can only be attributed to one of three things:

1. *The timing of the Lord;*
2. *The attack of the devil;*
3. *Personal laziness.*

When I see what God has entrusted to frail men and women who could say *yes* or *no*, it makes me love Him all the more. It makes me realize my frailty. I realize my tendency to say, "God, there are others who are much more equipped. They know the Word far better than I do. They have a greater anointing, ability, and sensitivity than I have." I find that many times my fear and insecurity hold me back from obeying God.

I'm tired. I think I need some Raisinets. Then, after I've been fortified, let's get going!

Eight

I Know I Haven't Arrived—but at Least I've Left!

I OFTEN poke fun at my Pentecostal roots and at being raised in the church doing silly things. I remember when my dad had all these campaigns to increase attendance in Sunday school. We had free doughnuts if you rode the bus, free bubblegum on Sunday, or the pastor would eat a raw egg in overalls on the church roof on Sunday morning. It's okay to laugh at some of the gimmicks that were used back then.

Yet there are some things that I will be forever grateful for in my roots. I am grateful that I was taught from the time I could speak that when you came to Jesus, He wasn't something you did part-time. You gave Him your whole life. Everything was His. Jesus was Lord. This walk was not for casual Christians. Another thing I am grateful for in my roots is that you were either in or out of the kingdom. You couldn't walk somewhere in between—couldn't straddle the fence.

One of the things that grieves the Holy Spirit is that there are so many who have one foot in the kingdom of God and one foot in the world.

The call of God is *weighing* on you. Jesus is saying, "I'm not asking you to walk the identical walk that I walked." Though He was a man, He is the Son of God. He's not asking you to go to the cross and pay the price He paid. He promised us that we would do greater things than He did. If we want that kind of power, we must have the same dedication to Him. We have to be *sold out* to Him.

If you do not know Jesus, I want to tell you that He is crazy about you. He is absolutely wildly and madly in love with you. He is not holding you back but is saying, "Come to Me. Come to Me. I want to change things for you. I love you and I want to lift your burden. I want to baptize you. I will turn the circumstances and situations around in your life." If you are coming from ground zero, you need to make a commitment now.

Some of you are 30 percenters. That's the first hurdle you have to cross. You're a Sunday morning, two-hour Christian. The problem is that if you are only a 30 percenter, 70 percent remains where the enemy is actively trying to get you to back off. You'll be a miserable believer because you'll have just enough of Jesus to know you need to do right, but not enough of Him to live a glorious, victorious life.

There are also 60 percenters. The problem with 60 percenters is that 40 percent of unsanctified flesh still remains within them. They have a little more of God; they pay their tithes and may even attend Wednesday night church. They may have a few praise-and-worship tapes interspersed with their new Kenny G and other secular CDs.

They're walking around asking why the devil is bombarding them. Why is it so difficult? They resemble those believers who look as if they were being chased by the devil continually. There is still that 40 percent of them that hasn't been committed to the Lord.

I love to sit at my piano, get out the old hymnal, and

sing, "Where He leads me I will follow; I'll go with Him, with Him, all the way." Then I sing, "I'll go with Him through the garden."

Do you know who has the anointing today? Do you know whom God is raising up today? Those who have said, "God, take all my earthly possessions. They're all Yours anyway. They don't mean anything to me. It's just stuff."

If you are like me, there are some areas where I am 100 percent in God; in some areas I'm still 60 percent, and in other areas I'm 30 percent. I'll be the first to admit that I am not 100 percent all the time. There are areas in my life where God is dealing with me and speaking to me. He's trying to work His work in me.

God's 100 Percenters

THAT LAST hurdle is the 100 percenter. Those are the people who are godly twenty-four hours a day. I don't know many people like that. Brother Arthur Burt is the only person I know of who actually fits that description. He gets translated. He shows up in places, and you don't even know how he got there, and you don't know how he left. He was once a servant to Smith Wigglesworth. He is still wearing the same light blue pants he bought in 1968. He still wears the zip-up sweater like your grandfather wears. And he plays the tambourine offbeat, up and down his arm. But he is wall-to-wall Jesus. He doesn't even fight the devil anymore.

I told him we needed to do more warfare. He said, "Cathy, you need to get in higher gear. You're riding around in second gear. You'll get there, but I'll get there first."

I have to have everything planned out every hour of every day. Brother Arthur just walks around serving God.

If you know you're not 100 percent in certain areas, no one needs to tell you—you just know. Everyone who has passed hurdle number two knows what is keeping them back from being 100 percent. It's comfortable to stay at 60 percent because there is a little bit of the blessing there.

There is some of the glory there. There are some little spiritual goosebumps there. We can sing and worship God. We can see God honoring us a little bit. There's some blessing.

However, the job of the prophet is to let the noise ring in your ear that your God is requiring something more of you. He wants you to do something greater than you've ever done, be someone greater than you've ever been, go a little further than you've ever gone, and give a little more than you've ever given.

To stay in the supernatural you must get over the last hurdle. It's called the mental hurdle. It's what we call the cares and passions of this world. "What fell among the thorns, these are [the people] who hear, but as they go on their way they are choked and suffocated with the anxieties and cares and riches and pleasures of life" (Luke 8:14, AMP).

I remember the day when we wouldn't dream of working on Sunday morning. It never entered our minds. Sunday was a holy day unto the Lord. "Well, Cathy, we're in a new hour. You just don't understand." You can't even repent unless He gives it to you. It takes an act of fasting.

Just a Few Words About Fasting...

I WANT to tell you something about fasting so you won't feel bad. He's pleased with whatever you give Him. How many of you have said, "I'm going to fast for three days"? Then about eleven o'clock on the first day of your fast you are in your kitchen, and all of a sudden you start getting woozy.

You hear the Holy Spirit say, "You need an Oreo."

You say, "Okay, God, I don't want to do this—but I just feel like You want me to." Then you have black crumbs all over your face. You stand there knowing you have eaten that Oreo, and all this condemnation says, *What a crummy Christian you are! You can't even fast for two hours!*

My dad and I often joke by saying we are going to fast between eleven and eleven-thirty. Laugh if you want to, but

God appreciates the effort you give Him—even if it's only thirty minutes.

I want to tell you something about the heart of my Father. As kind as He tells us to be to others, that's how kind He is to you.

Some of you have an image of God standing up there in heaven with a whip, ready to crack it over your head because He's so mad at you. But whip-cracking never saved anybody. It's the goodness of the Lord that brings someone to repentance. There are levels of position in eternity, and we are rewarded for what we've done on earth. God is telling us that He wants us to be valiant. He's training us to be valiant in His army because Zion is calling us to come up higher.

When I read the Word it's obvious to me that it makes no provision for losers. It makes no provision for failures. I can trust God. If a righteous man falls seven times but gets back up, He will not utterly cast him down, for the Lord upholds him with His hand.

Jesus can use a 30 percenter. He can use a 60 percenter. But the third hurdle is where the devil will swarm you with distractions. A secret that I've discovered in my life is that it's not the big mountains that give you the most trouble—it's all the little foothills. I can recognize the mountains. But I often miss the foothills until they're right in front of me. I just didn't see them coming.

WATCH OUT FOR THE DEVIL'S DISTRACTIONS

IF THE devil came to me and said, "Look at that construction worker out there, pulling his shirt off and drinking a Pepsi. Look at that big chest, those Tarzan boobies on that man," I would instantly know to cast that thought down. (I would look real fast just once.)

My husband will turn fifty this year. He's *much* older than I am. As we were walking around the hotel pool in our bathing suits one day I told him that I was going to throw him a big party. He said he didn't want one.

I was trying to cheer him up, so I told him that Arnold Schwarzenegger just turned fifty—and look at him! My husband stopped, looked at me, and said, "Thank you very much."

I told him I really didn't mean anything by my remark. "I was just showing you what you could be at fifty."

He gave me "that" look and said, "I'm going back to the room."

The devil will swarm you with distractions. This is where the deceitfulness of riches and the love of money come in. You will be distracted with things—beautiful things. Satan will try to find something quite enticing to keep you from being 100 percent for God.

Not only do you want to, but God wants you to be 100 percent for Him. The devil's object is to neutralize the Word that is in you. He will use the deceitfulness of riches and financial pressure to take the Word from you so you will say, "That's good, but I just don't know how I'm going to pay the bills."

God wants to take some of you on mission trips. He wants to use some of you to fund mission trips. He's calling you to a higher place. Financial pressure has the ability to change a man. However, when God begins to bless your ability to give, it will change you. It will change how you feel about yourself.

Just remember that Jesus is your true treasure. For some of you, money comes to you, and you get distracted. You have to separate yourself from glamour and the pressure of money, cares, and other anxieties associated with temporary things. If we have learned anything, we know that all that stuff can go up in smoke in a moment of time.

I remember a little poem we used to say when I was a child: "Only one life, 'twill soon be past. Only what's done for Christ will last." Separate yourself. Make time to be alone with God and pray and grow and stretch. Jesus said He would give the most to those who could best manage what they had.

YES, BUT CAN GOD TRUST YOU?

BELIEVER AFTER believer has cried at the altar, "Lord, I want more." Yet, if you were to follow them around all week, you would hear them murmur about what they already have. With greater increase of anointing comes greater blessing.

God couldn't trust some of you with greater financial blessing because you would lose your simplicity. You'd get distracted. You may not fully realize it, but He knows the secret places of your heart.

Our God tells us that He gives the most to those who can best manage what they have. He's not keeping it *from* you; He's keeping it *for* you. So make room for a greater blessing. If you are doing that, you must also make room for greater responsibility. With greater blessing comes greater responsibility.

My husband and I look at our precious daughter Jerusha and think of that song, "Butterfly Kisses." We must have done something right. Randi and I look at her and marvel. She has the most guileless spirit toward the things of the Lord. She has never rebelled or raised her fist against us.

I say that in order to say this: She has a Mazda. When Jerusha is driving and I am the passenger, she will pull right up to the bumper of the car ahead before she stops. I have even helped her brake the car by stomping the floor of the car and grabbing my "Jesus-help-me" handle.

I yell at her to slow down and not slam on the brakes. She says, "Mother, you make me so nervous! Dad doesn't make me nervous. He says you're the kind of driver that causes accidents because you stop a mile before the car is there." That's right—I'm the kind of mother that tells her not to flash her lights or look at people in other cars because they may be crazy and have a gun.

One day Jerusha was late getting back from the office. I couldn't reach her on her car phone, and I was getting concerned. When she finally walked in the door, her eyes were red from crying. I was sitting propped up on my bed, and all I said was, "What!"

She ran over to me and said, "I had an accident! I rear-ended someone. It was just a fender-bender, honest."

I went out and looked at the car. The engine was in the trunk. Something rose up within me. I wanted to yell, "I just told you yesterday not to tailgate! Who's going to pay for this? We have a deductible, you know."

Before I could say any of this, she threw herself at my feet and began to sob. "Mom, I am so sorry. I know I was wrong. Please forgive me. I'll do whatever it takes. I'll work without pay; I'll make up the difference; I'll do anything you ask."

Everything that was stuck in my throat ready to come out didn't need to be said because Jerusha threw herself on my mercy and repented. All I wanted to do was put my arms around her and comfort her. We began to pray in the Spirit. I thanked God for protecting her. We stood against the spirit of fear.

Then I said, "Honey, what was the worst thing about this accident?"

She said, "Well, I guess when I was standing on Southside and everyone was coming by and staring at me—that was the worst part."

Randi was out of the country. After we were through praying, Jerusha said, "Mom, do you think it's really necessary to tell Dad?" I told her he was the high priest of our house and her father. She said, "I think the Lord told me that we could have the car fixed and get it back before he gets home."

She didn't tell her father about the accident when he called. Her excuse was that her hands had started to sweat and her mouth had gotten dry. She said she took that as a sign from the Lord that she shouldn't say anything. She said she didn't want to burden him while he was out there in the mission field ministering. Another sign.

Eventually she told him. She was glad because, as she told me later, "He wasn't hardly mad."

That's just how it is with our heavenly Father when we throw ourselves upon His mercy. We discover, much to our surprise, that He "isn't hardly mad." He loves us too much for that.

God's Call to Come Up Higher

IN LUKE 15 we read about the prodigal son. I know you have heard many sermons on the prodigal son, but I want to tell you my slant on this to tie in with God calling us to a higher place in Him.

The prodigal son did not lack for stuff. Everything the father had was his. In the same way Prince Charles, as the son of the queen of England, gets anything he wants. One day when Charles and Diana were courting, he wanted to buy her something at a soccer game. He didn't count the change out correctly because he never carried money. Things were always taken care of for him. (I read this story in a magazine, and I know it is true. If you can't trust the *National Enquirer,* whom *can* you trust?) Charles wasn't a poor man; he was very wealthy. He just didn't sign his own checks.

The prodigal son wasn't poor either. He was wealthy. His father wasn't stingy. When the son asked for his portion, his father gave it to him. The difference was that the prodigal son did not have control of his portion.

One of the things that will keep you from being a 100 percenter is when you insist on having control. The prodigal wanted control. He didn't want to have to go to his father.

After he left his father's house, for a short season it still looked as if he had all that stuff. There are some of you whose hearts are far from the Lord. Yet you go to church and praise and worship. You wave your hands in the air because you like the music. Yet you have long since left the Father's house and have taken control of your own lives.

I remember a time in my life when I ceased to obey God. I knew I was living in pure grace. God was blessing me, but I knew that if I didn't stop what I was doing and get back into obedience, all that grace was going to come to a quick, sudden end.

There is a season that we can ride in God's extended mercy, but if we do not get back in the Father's house it will come to an end. Some of you are riding on the grace of God, but you know you have long since stopped obeying Him. You are not walking in that 100 percent He has called you to walk in.

The sad part is that the prodigal returned home after sitting among pigs. Being a Jew, that was the bottom-of-the-pit thing for him to do. In his independent spirit he chose his own path without consideration of what it might ultimately cost him to do so.

He decided to return home. His father brought out the fatted calf to be killed and roasted in his honor, put a robe and ring on him, and tossed a big party. However, I have never read where the prodigal ever received another inheritance.

God is so faithful toward us. Great is His faithfulness. He loves us and takes us back. Yet we read in His Word that once a king has fallen, he is never restored to that place of kingship again.

We have seen many in the body of Christ who have been given great honor. They left the Father's house and rode for a while on God's grace. Then their entire world fell apart. Even though many of them have been restored to ministry, their names will always be associated with shame, reproach, and dishonor.

A Word of Warning

I BELIEVE there is a word of warning to some of you who have let things slide. The Spirit of the Lord is calling you up higher. I believe there is a word of encouragement to you.

You are at a crossroad, and you are going to have to say *yes* or *no* to Him right now. You are going to have to say, "Lord, I am going on," or "Lord, I am going to live as a 60 percenter and hang on to what I have right now." There are areas of your life where you must stop telling God, "You can have this, this, and this—but don't You dare touch *this* area. I reserve the right to have *this* for myself."

Oh, that I might know Him and the power of His resurrection! But I can only have *fellowship* with Him in His sufferings.

Zion is calling you up higher.

Make a declaration that you will never be the same. I don't care if you have walked with Jesus for a long time or if this is the first time you have heard of Him—the voice of the prophet is ringing in your ear.

The Lord says, "I have more for you. You have to come in more frequently to Me. If you want what you've never had before, you've got to do what you've never done before."

It begins with dedicating *all that you are* to Him.

Nine

"What Do You Mean, My Brook Has Dried Up?"

T HE very word that Elijah prophesied had come to pass, and not only did it bring drought upon the land but it caused his own provision to dry up too.

> And he drank of the brook. And it came to pass after a while, that the brook dried up, because there had been no rain in the land.
>
> —1 Kings 17:6–7

Has God ever given you a word that says, "I am going to use you. You are going to preach and minister, and I'm going to put finances into your hand"?

YES! But the next thing you know . . . your brook has dried up. What do you have? Things got worse instead of better. Everything went contrary to what God said. *What kind of God is this?* He sends the prophet to a place of security and provision; then He lets it all dry up.

God does that, you know. He brings us to places, jobs, situations, people, even to businesses for seasons in our lives. Then suddenly we find that we must do battle. In the midst of believing God to do all the things He has promised to do, it seems as if our brook dries up. Did it ever occur to you that God knows something we don't know? He knows that if He doesn't dry it up, we will stay there and worship at the brook. He knows that if He doesn't dry up the brook, we will never move forward to the next place He has prepared for us.

The brook did provide refreshing water for Elijah for a season. It was God's perfect will for him . . . for a while. However, it wasn't a forever thing.

THE TIME OF RESTORATION IS NOW

PROPHECY IS not going to go out of style. Someone told me, "Yeah, I know all about prophecy. I was in that at one time, and now I'm doing something else." Prophecy is the heart and mind of God being spoken through the mouths of His prophets. It is not going to be out of fashion.

> Behold, I will send you Elijah the prophet before the coming of the great and dreadful day of the LORD: And he shall turn the heart of the fathers to the children, and the heart of the children to their fathers, lest I come and smite the earth with a curse.
> —MALACHI 4:5–6

To all you parents who have children from another marriage or whose children are grown, I prophesy to you that you are about to come into a wonderful hour in the church of the Lord Jesus. Those of you who have prayed, stood, and believed are going to see the restoration of grown children. You are going to see them coming back to the Lord. To those who have family members who haven't spoken to each other for a long time, I prophesy that there will be a restoration of families.

The Elijah ministry is a ministry of restoration. This is the season of restoration. God is restoring the church. Jesus was the greater Elijah. The spirit of Elijah is a prophetic-word anointing. What does that mean?

Most of you are aware that the first baby we adopted, Hannah Ruth, is black. One day an intercessor came to me and said, "The Lord spoke to me and told me to pray for Hannah." I thought she meant my girlfriend, but she said God had a word for Hannah Ruth *Lechner*.

And here is what that intercessor said: "As I began to pray for Hannah, I saw her at about ten years old, standing, preaching to countries that were war torn, prophesying the Word of the Lord. The Lord told me that she is special and that He has His hand on her. That's why she is so advanced for her age." Glory!

God is going to use our children at young ages so we won't have to wait. Those of you who are believing God for your teenagers are not going to have to go through years of rebellious kids if you do it right. I firmly believe in disciplining children. (I have a twenty-year-old daughter who is living proof that it works.)

The Spirit of Elijah

WHAT KIND of man was Elijah? The Word says the spirit— the anointing—of Elijah will be on the earth today. We don't know anything about Elijah before he is mentioned in 1 Kings 17:1: "And Elijah the Tishbite, who was of the inhabitants of Gilead, said unto Ahab, As the LORD God of Israel liveth, before whom I stand, there shall not be dew nor rain these years, but according to my word." But from that moment on, we see a clear picture of Elijah's character. He emerges as a man who stands for truth, speaks the truth, and boldly proclaims the Word of the Lord as the Spirit of the Lord directs him to do so.

This fiery prophet marched in before Ahab and began to prophesy the Word of the Lord, regardless of what might happen to him as a result. I assume you have to have a vivid imagination to make that exciting. So although we don't know anything about his background, we know from Scripture that Elijah walked in fearlessly before the king and began to prophesy judgment. Here was a man who did not suffer from fear and timidity.

The thing that will hinder you and me from pressing in and moving out into the things that God has for us is a spirit of fear and timidity. Some excuses are: "I don't want to do it because I'm afraid of what they will say." Or, "I'm too old, too young, too thin, too fat, too tall. I can't walk too well, so maybe somebody else ought to do it."

Granted, there are some prophets who are "out of balance" and go off the deep end. But as a general rule, we prophets are more afraid of *moving out* than of being as bold as Elijah.

When Randi and I were pastoring, I decided to hold a women's conference. This was before such conferences were popular and plentiful. We formed a committee and knew it would be a real step of faith. I lay in bed at night wondering if we could do it financially. I prayed, "Lord, I don't want to displease You. I don't want to be frivolous and waste Your money."

The Lord spoke to me and said, "Cathy, I own it all. I'd rather you choose *yes* in faith than to say *no* in fear." I knew then that it is faith, not fear, that pleases God.

We don't know what it took to prepare Elijah. God had entrusted him with a great task of honor. He stood before his mountain, fearless. On the mountaintop were five hundred prophets of Baal who would try every trick in the book to turn the peoples' hearts away from God. It was Elijah's task to display God's power openly for all to see.

God's School

COMPLETE FEARLESSNESS and confidence in the Lord—that's what God is after. Some of you listen to the news every night and are frightened. Even though I assure my mother that my car doors lock automatically, she is always reminding me to lock them, look straight ahead when driving, have my car phone in my hand at all times, wear clean underwear in case of an accident, and remember never to talk to strangers. Now that's what I call a spirit of fear. God's going after that spirit of fear. He wants to replace it with a spirit of boldness.

We need to be in the "School of the Spirit." That's where every confidence of the flesh is cut away. We must let God perform surgery on us and cut away everything in which we had confidence in the past.

I know firsthand about the dealings of God in a life. I call such a place the "Pit of God's Dealing." Everyone would like to do great and mighty things for the Lord. But how many would offer to start with cleaning the church toilets and mopping the floors? The way we come into greatness in the kingdom of God is through humility and brokenness.

Sometimes we have to come crawling or we will hit our heads. We have to say, "I don't care if I'm ever famous. It doesn't make any difference to me if I ever go anywhere or if anyone ever knows my name. All I want to do is walk in a manner that is pleasing to You and hear You say, 'Well done, thou good and faithful servant.'"

Before God can take us before the pharaohs and the Ahabs of the world, there must always be a period of preparation in obscurity. There must be a period of preparation where it looks like, "All I ever do is die. All I ever do is give in. I'm always the one; I've got to pull the whole load. I have to do all the praying. This family wouldn't even go to church if it weren't for me. I'm the one. I give and give and give, but I never have any testimonies of someone walking up to me and giving *me* money. I just don't understand."

Even Jesus had to walk through those places. Except for His birth and bar mitzvah, we don't read anything more about Jesus until He was thirty years old. Until then He lived with Mary and Joseph in Nazareth in relative obscurity, and I imagine He measured and cut wood, went for water, and did all the mundane things that were expected of Him as a boy growing up.

The Spirit of the Lord will use many mundane things in our lives to prepare us. He will use our marriages, ministry, failures, finances, and even that job we absolutely hate to go to every day. We are crying out, "Lord, release me from this place!" But God is using the very things we can't tolerate to shape us and conform us to the image of Christ. It's called the sandpaper of the Holy Spirit.

After going through God's school, Elijah stood before Ahab and boldly prophesied the Word of the Lord.

> Ahab the son of Omri did evil in the sight of the LORD, more than all who were before him. And it came to pass, as though it had been a trivial thing for him to walk in the sins of Jeroboam the son of Nebat, that he took as wife Jezebel.
>
> —1 KINGS 16:30, NKJV

As if Ahab didn't have enough problems, he married Jezebel. Many people think that the problem with her was that she wore too much makeup. That wasn't it at all. Her problem was that she was a manipulating and controlling female. She dominated, manipulated, and controlled, using much emotion and intimidation in order to have her own way.

If you are going to be used of God, you cannot have that kind of spirit. Do you know that the Jezebel spirit can be disguised as very sweet? Ahab was worse than all the kings who had gone before him. Jezebel single-handedly killed all the prophets in the land. Do you know why? She couldn't stand anyone speaking the truth! That is a strong characteristic of the Jezebel spirit.

How many times have you heard someone say, "Walk on eggshells around her because if you cross her, there's hell to pay." And it's not just women who may have that Jezebel spirit. There are many men with that same spirit.

I have been in services where a prophetic word was given with such anger that I thought the prophet was going to strike the person he was talking to. It's as if he were trying to bring down God's wrath on the poor soul. Didn't he know that it is written that "*God so loved* the world that He gave . . . "? The key words there are *God so loved.*

Back to bold Elijah! He stood before the most black-hearted king who had ever lived. Ahab did more to provoke God than all of his ancestors put together. There were seven thousand faithful believers who hadn't bowed their knees to Baal, but Elijah was the only prophet left. Jezebel had killed the rest of them.

Even though Ahab was rotten to the core, God sent Elijah to him. Some of you have been saying, "Surely God wouldn't want me to stay in this rotten job! These people are such heathens." Or, "God wouldn't expect me to live with this person! He's so awful." But why do you suppose God has allowed you to stay where you are? Could it be that you are there to be a witness for the Lord?

The first words that Elijah said were, "As the Lord, the God of Israel, lives." I believe Elijah's entire life was based on that statement.

In order for you and me to walk into what God has for us, we have to determine once and for all that, "Because He lives, He lives *in* me and *for* me. He is concerned with every detail of my life. He loves me. He is restoring me. I stand as a person who is wrapped up in the Father, the Son, and the Holy Spirit. I stand in the anointing and can speak boldly of what He will do because He has already paid the price for me."

Elijah wasn't being arrogant. He walked in both boldness and humility. He said, "I'm going to die—I just *know* I'm going to die." But Elijah knew it would not be him speaking to Ahab, but *God through him.*

The shaping of a vessel such as Elijah is not accomplished in one day, a week, or at one conference. I'd like you to say aloud, "I know that I haven't arrived, but at least I've started the journey."

First Corinthians 6:17 says, "But he who is joined to the Lord is one spirit" (NKJV). If Elijah had not been so joined with the Lord, he would have not obeyed His instructions.

But following his mountaintop experience in which he called down fire from heaven and killed the prophets of Baal, Elijah was exhausted. Something that he would ordinarily have taken in stride—a death threat from Jezebel—caused him to run to the wilderness.

The Word tells us that Elijah was fed there by ravens. Those birds that eat out of garbage dumps were sent to take care of his hunger. He could have said, "Those birds are unclean, so they can't be of God." He may even have thought, *It's a satanic plot to destroy my life.*

AWESOME FEARLESSNESS

HAS GOD ever used something impossible to confront your fear? A girl in one of my meetings said to me, "Cathy, the first time you came to our city you ministered to us. You gave us an *awesome* word. We were rejoicing all the way home. The next time you came you prophesied, 'Your job is not your source, and God says, "I will provide for you."'" I went home and sobbed for three days. I was angry because for the first time in our lives we had great paying jobs, were finally out of debt, and were able to afford the things we needed. Two weeks later, my husband's company went out of business. We lost our jobs. *The word of the Lord that we received through you sustained us during that difficult time.*"

There are many ways the devil will choose to torment you. *What if I have to be alone? What if God doesn't . . . ?* You'll live through those things, and God will show His strength in the middle of them all. He will provide and show you His goodness. You confessed all your faith, said all the right words, stood on the Word of the Lord, and when you opened your eyes it didn't happen. But it was still God right in the center of it all, and He showed Himself strong for you. He is more interested in changing *you* than He is in using you to change everyone else.

We all love security. A few years ago we had a two-bedroom house. We converted our garage into a third bedroom. I had infants climbing the walls. It looked as if I were running a Humpty Dumpty Day Care Center. The house was so small you almost had to go outside to change your mind. I couldn't put my desk anywhere because I needed the room for a playpen and a swing. We had to hunt the high chair when we needed it, and the bouncy thing babies like was stored under the table when not in use.

Someone prophesied to me that God was going to provide us with a larger home. I believed in my heart that was true, but something in me wanted to hang on to this home . . . and my security. *What if we move and the roof leaks? What if we move and after a month I don't like it? What if I can't make the payments?* What if . . . what if . . . what *if?*

What I didn't want to admit was that I felt secure in my little house. At least I knew everything there was to know about this one. There is something about security that will cause us to hang on to our raisin when God has a watermelon for us if we will just trust Him. I had my raisin—my little house—but I knew I had to let it go in order for God to give me the watermelon—a larger one.

God is taking us to places in Him that we have never been before. God is stirring us up and doing things in ministry. He's doing what you and I asked Him to do.

But first He will dry up your brook. So you have a choice:

You can sit by the brook and say, "I bind this satanic thing. When I open my eyes I will no longer be in this barren place but in a nice green valley where there is water!"

You can stare at your dried-up brook and prophesy until your voice gives out that it's going to run with water once again. Or you can move with the Spirit to the new place the Lord has prepared for you. You've been binding and rebuking over and over again—and losing the anointing in the process. That brook still ran dry. Could it possibly be that God is in this thing? How do you know for sure? By repeated hearing and obedience. God does not want you concentrating on the brook for your provision. The whole desire and heart of God is that you look to Him for all your provision. So don't concentrate on that job, ministry, provision, or the one who broke that promise to you.

Don't focus on the provision. When it is time and the brook dries up, God will direct you to the next place of His supply. He says, "Arise; I have different provision, ministry, anointing, different circumstances, other people to feed you, and another place to use you."

LIVING ON THE EDGE

SOMETIMES WALKING this faith walk means "dangling." It's living on the edge of faith where God is either going to come through or we are all doing to die. (At least that's what it *feels* like!)

I've been told, "Cathy, you don't understand! It's easy for you because you are in the ministry and you have a Christian husband." *Huh?* I think not. I have said repeatedly, "New levels bring new devils." The higher you go in Him, the more fierce the battle.

What is God drying up in your life? What have you been worshiping? Where are you worshiping? You may be saying, "I can't take this situation any longer. If You don't do something soon, I'm going to die." You have been worshiping at the altar of your marriage.

Why not say, "Lord, I'm going to serve You whether Buster serves You or not. I'm going to love You even if Herb watches television all the time and gets mad because I'm going to church. At least one of us in this house is going to be happy." Or, "Lord, You've been speaking to me about the mission field. I've been hanging on because the economy is going down, and I have things to take care of. Lord, I'm going to obey You now. I know You will provide."

I want to inspire you to let the Spirit of God light your fire today. I desire for Him to stir you in areas that you have been discouraged in. You may be thinking, *When God does this one thing,* then *I will go, or when the Lord does that other thing,* then *I'll be able to go.*

The hour is *now*. Do what He wants you to do. Say to Him, "Lord, whatever You want me to do, I will do it. If it is Your desire that I stay right here at this brook just a while longer and worship and love You, my answer is, 'Yes, Lord.' If Your desire is for me to stay home and be the best housewife and mother and love these kids and my husband, my answer is yes to that as well. I will do whatever You ask of me."

Whatever you have now is what God can trust you with. The more you obey, the more you walk with God, the more He will entrust to you.

Father, we will hear and obey!

Ten

RUN TO THE BATTLE

I'M looking for a voice. I know you blew it, and you haven't been perfect. You've gotten busy and distracted and missed your prayer time many times. But I know that you love Me, and I'm looking for a voice to speak in the earth today."

That's what I keep hearing the Spirit of the Lord say over and over again.

I was in the mall parking lot, just about to park by the store where I intended to buy Erin, my secretary, a birthday gift. I was strongly impressed to drive to the other side of the store to park. As I pulled into the parking space, again I felt impressed that I was in the wrong space, so I moved forward to another one. I knew it was the prompting of the Holy Spirit to move my car, so I obeyed.

As I got out of my car I noticed a girl struggling to get into her car. I asked her if I could help, perhaps call someone for her. She stared at me and asked, "Are you Cathy Lechner?"

My first response was *going* to be, "Are you a bill collector just pretending to get into your car so you could serve me for something? If you are, just go back home."

Before I could answer she said, "I can't get into my car, and I can't find my AAA card. Someone came around and asked if they could help, but they wanted twenty-five dollars."

The Lord spoke to me and said, "Give her the twenty-five dollars." I obeyed the Lord. She promised she would repay me, but I refused and told her that God had arranged this meeting.

"Are you a backslider?" I asked her.

"Yes, I am. I used to attend church, but I walked away from God. When I moved, I got away from counsel and got involved with a man." In that cold, windy parking lot I held that girl in my arms and began to prophesy the Word of the Lord to her. I guess we looked rather odd as people passed by and saw a black girl and a white lady hugging and crying in the parking lot of the mall.

That day God was looking for a voice, someone who didn't mind making a fool of themselves in public to reach out to one of His little ones. I told her I was speaking in Ohio that weekend, but I would be back in time to go to church, even if I had to go directly from the airport. I would be willing to do that if she would agree to meet me there and give her heart back to the Lord. She gave me her promise.

On Sunday morning there she was, sitting in the back of the church waiting for the altar call. How exciting to walk up that aisle with her. The Spirit of the Lord touched her that day in a very special way.

God Is Looking for Amateurs

YOU DON'T have to say, "Thus saith the Lord." All you have

to do is to be available for Him to use. God's cry has always been, "Give me a widow, a widower, a divorcée. Give me someone who will speak for me." God is not looking for professionals. He's looking for amateurs! That's the category I fit in.

You see, if you wait until you become a professional to become the voice of the Lord, you will have a set way of doing things that excludes the Spirit of God using you for any kind of ministry.

Don't you often wish that when God called you and hands were laid on you that you received everything you needed to be totally changed for the rest of your life? No more problems with your flesh, no more problems finding time to pray. You would always be on a spiritual countdown, ready to launch. You'd have it all together for the rest of your life.

But when Samuel anointed David to be king, it did not happen overnight. Even after being anointed by Samuel, David didn't do everything God had planned for him to do immediately, but he was still anointed to rule Israel. It took seventeen years before the words that were prophesied to him by Samuel came to pass. (That's the part I have a problem with. When I get a word from the Lord, I want it to come to pass the minute I walk out the door of the church.) But God had to prepare David for what he was destined to become.

THE ANOINTED ONE WITHIN

SAY ALOUD with me: "I'm anointed because the Anointed One is with me." He doesn't care how many times you've failed. He doesn't care if you stand up in church and tell what an awesome thing God did in your life and then turn around the next day and blow it again. The Anointed One is with you whether you have been a believer for two days, two years, or two hundred years. The Anointed One is with you.

Everyone has his or her own personal battle. Sometimes the Lord will bring a crisis into your life just to bring you to a closer place in Him. There are many men and women of God who can look back upon a particular crisis in their lives and remember that as the place where they felt the greatest anointing.

How you deal with your crisis will depend on how far you will be able to go in the Spirit. Have you ever dealt with a crisis and handled it all wrong? I can look back at the battles I have had to face when I had to decide which way I would go. Many of you are in a battle for your marriage, children, ministry, finances, or business. You are discouraged and want to retreat or run. You have to pray and choose which path to take because your desire is to be obedient.

It was when I was fighting those battles that I pressed closer to the Lord. There were times when I would bang my head against the shower wall and say, "I can't, Lord; I can't."

But the Lord would answer, "Yes, you can. Yes, you can." That's when the grace of God kicks in and helps you do what you are unable to do in your own flesh. In situations where you think you just can't possibly win, God does wonders.

DAVID AND GOLIATH

GOLIATH CALLED and David responded. This was David's first major battle, the one that would propel him to the forefront. Up to that moment he had been devalued by everyone. When Samuel came to anoint a king, David wasn't even considered a candidate by his father and his brothers. Talk about rejection! However, God put a premium on David's life. The prophet sent for him. David's family didn't even give him a thought. If they were in today's world they surely would have been in an episode of Montel Williams called, "My Brothers Hated Me, and Now They're Really Sorry."

Have you ever been devalued by family members who thought you would never amount to anything? Has the devil devalued you to yourself because of something in your past? Perhaps you failed, and you felt as if you were just a nobody. Let me tell you, friend, the Anointed One is with you. He will never devalue you.

When Samuel did not find a king in the midst of the sons of Jesse, the prophet asked if there were any more sons not present. This is what he was told: "There is just one other son, but he smells like sheep droppings." Never in their wildest dreams did David's family think that God could use the likes of a shepherd boy. That attitude prevailed toward David even after Jesse and his sons saw Samuel pour oil upon the young boy's head and proclaim him king.

When David brought food to his brothers in the battlefield, they questioned his presence there. David must have been in la-la land because I don't think what his brothers thought bothered him. He had just come from the shepherd's field where he communed with God and sang praises to Him. What a wonderful place to be!

I could never understand why the armies of Israel didn't just get together and "rush" Goliath. If one of us can put a thousand to flight and two ten thousand, why couldn't the Israelites just gang up on that big bully? But we understand that God was in charge of this situation, just as He is in every situation.

David had confidence in God. This battle between David and Goliath is often used as a Sunday school story. But please understand, this was a real battle. It was also a spiritual battle, as are most of ours. Are you having a problem in finances? It's a spiritual battle. Are you being tested in ministry? It's a spiritual battle. Most of the battles we face are spiritual. We must have the same confidence in God that David had so we that can face that giant and say, "Who is this uncircumcised Philistine?"

The Word tells us that our battle is not against flesh and blood but against principalities, powers, and rulers of darkness. Battles may fall into different categories, but it is still the same devil we are warring against. Can't pay the electric bill? One category. Cancer! Another category. No matter what the category, we must be like David—*confident!*

God does His best work when we are in a no-win situation. We are told by well-meaning believers, "Just stand in faith! Rise up in faith!" Easy to say, isn't it? But when I had to deal with our adopted son Joshua's illness, I found out that it wasn't all that easy to do. I knew what God *could* do, but I just didn't know *when* or *how* He would do it. (There's a lot of stuff from the faith movement that they forgot to tell us.)

By experience I had to learn many new things about walking by faith. I knew that I was in uncharted territory when what I confessed didn't come to pass. Even though I didn't understand, it was still my battle, my giant.

How to Win

How DID David win this no-win battle against Goliath? He nurtured his faith. He spent time alone with his God. We have to look at what David had been doing up until the point of the battle. What you are doing up until the point of your battle will determine when and how and at what level God will take you in. It will set your course.

I know of several mighty men of God who at one time were unheard of because God had them hidden away. He was preparing them for battle, preparing them to go to a new level. Men and women we have never heard of have suddenly come forward and are being used prophetically by God in our time.

You may feel that you are hidden away and that your promise is not coming to pass. Remember, God is preparing you. He is always at work.

Where was David up until this time? He was out tending the sheep . . . alone. I wish I could tell you there is an easier way. I'd like to tell you that through some instantaneous process faith will zap you and carry you through for the rest of your life.

But that's not so. The journey is long and upward in nature. Just when I get to the top and breathe a sigh of relief, God shows me another peak just ahead and tells me, "Come on! We're going higher!"

I often get wonderful prophetic words that say, "I'm going to raise you up, and you are going to speak to kings—you're going to prophesy to the millennium. You'll be martyred for Me, but it won't hurt. You can have a potato chip while they are killing you." (Something like that!)

In the back of my mind I'm thinking, *There's a price; there's a price for God's glory!*

Solitude is not just sitting alone in the presence of God, chanting, "Ohhmn." Solitude is having that quiet time before the Spirit of God. There is a relationship that is developed during those quiet times. It's communication. We are so distracted today with all that is around us.

David spent a large portion of his life preparing himself before he ever walked into the battle. We look at this battle between David and Goliath as a miracle. But God gave him Goliath. It wasn't as much a miracle as it was a process that David had elected to go through prior to the battle, when the giant was given into his hand. His relationship with God is what had guaranteed his victory over the Philistine giant.

God puts His people through a process. You and I must be willing to prepare ourselves for the battles ahead. I will share with you that about 99 percent of the time in my life I do not have a clear-cut word from the Lord about the next step I am to take and the decision that I am about to make. I submit things to God, but He seems to open His will little by little as I take each step. I just do what comes next, and as I move forward a little bit more of God's plan for me unfolds.

When I found out about our adopted son Joshua's condition, I didn't want to go out and minister. The doctors told us that because he was born with most of his brain missing he would be blind, unable to walk, and would require constant medical care. Randi said, "Get up and go minister." I kept saying *no* because I didn't feel like it. I wanted to lay in bed and cry. I wanted to mourn. "Just give me a Coke and a *National Enquirer* and leave me alone."

I told Randi, "Honey, you have an anointing to provoke people." The Word says we're to "consider one another to provoke unto love and to good works" (Heb. 10:24). I can tell you that my husband walks very anointed in that gifting. He provokes people to love and good works. And he was doing that to me. I didn't want to go. I felt pitiful. I didn't want to face anyone, and I certainly didn't want to minister.

But as I submitted my emotions and my will to God He empowered me to keep moving on with God. And as I did, He provided the answers for little Joshua.

Through our attorney we were able to make contact with Joshua's biological family. We discovered that they had been praying for God to restore Joshua to their family. Though it was one of the hardest things Randi and I have ever had to do, we returned Joshua to his loving, biological family who is providing him with all the love and medical care that he needs as well as a loving church family.

David put one foot in front of another and kept moving on with God. That's what I want to encourage you to do. Encourage yourself. Stand! Don't run away from your battle. Pastor Wiley, my pastor, says it so beautifully: "God wants to give you a new appreciation for trials."

When I first heard that I thought, *That's just the devil, Pastor. I'm going to cast that thing out. Just cough!* Those two words, *appreciation* and *trials,* do not belong in the same sentence.

I do know that God wants to give us that appreciation. We need the kind of faith that is nurtured. It was the same thing that gave David strength in the midst of conflict. Saul told David, "You are not able to go out against this Philistine and fight him; you are only a boy, and he has been a fighting man from his youth" (1 Sam. 17:33, NIV).

But David answered him, "Your servant has been keeping his father's sheep. When a lion or a bear came and carried off a sheep from the flock, I went after it, struck it and rescued the sheep from its mouth. When it turned on me, I seized it by its hair, struck it and killed it . . . this uncircumcised Philistine will be like one of them, because he has defied the armies of the living God" (vv. 34–36, NIV).

In other words, David was telling Saul that Goliath was just another animal to him. Do you think the trial you are going through resembles Goliath? Let me tell you—your giant is just another animal!

What did winning those two battles do to build such confidence and strength into David? It strengthened David's faith because he had won these small battles. We often feel so sorry for ourselves, and the first thing we want to do is run and hide from our battles.

DON'T RUN: STAY AND FIGHT!

WHEN YOUR battles come, don't be surprised or shocked. My tendency when everything is going great is to say, "Everything is going so good, I'd better not enjoy this because something is going to happen to ruin everything. I haven't had a trial in a while. I just know the devil is sniffing around me. Something is going to happen."

David had faith and confidence when the giant came. To him this haughty Philistine was no different than the lion or the bear. We feel sorry for ourselves. Some of us are struggling with the small battles. How can we win the big ones if we are still struggling with the small battles? Don't run away from the small battles. The giants will come, and whether you succeed or fail with the giants in your life depends on whether you are willing to fight the lions and bears of the earlier battles.

"Oh, Lancelot!"

WE PRAY, "Oh, Lord, give me strength for the battle." The Lord spoke to me one night through a movie and told me, "You don't get strength *for* the battle; you get strength *from* the battle."

I was watching the movie against my will because I was very tired, having just returned from a conference. However, my daughter convinced me to stay up and watch a video with her. It was a love story called *First Knight*, the story of Camelot. I thought there was music in it, but she informed me it was "just talking."

I seem to derive something spiritual from everything that I see, and this was no exception. Lancelot, played by Richard Gere, had no passion for anything. King Arthur, portrayed by Sean Connery, wanted Lancelot to "come fight with us. Come serve at the round table." But Lancelot would not commit. Then something happened—someone whom Richard Gere really loved got touched. Unfortunately, it was someone else's wife. We now find a man who had no passion to fight for anything except money—that is, until something that was dear to him was on the line. At that moment he pulled out his sword and began to fight fiercely.

Lord, that's what it is! I thought. Lancelot didn't just poke at the enemy; he whacked them with his sword. Then he got two swords. I thought, *That's how it is in the Spirit. We don't get strength until we rise up and get into the fight. We don't get strength* for *it; we get strength* from *it.*

God wants you to rise up and press into the battle. Norman Schwarzkopf was getting ready to take us into the Persian Gulf during the Gulf War. Everyone kept asking, "Are we ready now? Are we going in?" The general kept putting them off. Everyone wondered what he was doing. He was studying the former battles that the United States had been involved in. He was looking for weaknesses, wrong decisions, and strategies that were not right. He didn't want to repeat past mistakes. And he was successful.

General Schwarzkopf looked back. So often we don't want to look back at the former battles. We want relief, rest, and we don't want to talk about it. We become spiritual Scarlett O'Haras—you know, "I'll think about it tomorrow."

But from time to time we need to look back and learn from our mistakes so that when we go into battle again we can say, "If God did that for me then, He'll do it for me now." If we have no battle experience, when the next giant comes on the scene we will go under.

"I HATE TRIALS: HOW ABOUT YOU?"

I'M NOT crazy about trials. I don't like battles. But if we don't have any battle experience, when we go through these things, we won't be able to stand. We will be discouraged, lose faith and hope, and go under.

David had faith that was proven in hopelessness. Do you know that hope deferred makes your heart sick? The other side of that coin is, "But a longing fulfilled is a tree of life" (Prov. 13:12, NIV). This means that if you hope long enough, even though your heart is sick, the word will come to pass. It will eventually be a tree of life to you.

To the casual observer the situation was hopeless; there was no way that David could possibly win. Everything was stacked against him. But he did win.

The beauty of the battle between David and Goliath is that God won the battle for him. The beauty of your battle is that when you win, you can't take any of the credit. All the glory goes to God.

When our daughter Jerusha faces trials I tell her, "Jerusha, I am holding on to you. There is no way I am letting you go. I'm hanging on to you." And that's what God does. He hangs on to us and doesn't let go. When *our* ability stops, God takes over and makes all of His limitless ability available to us.

God wants us to be willing to do things that reach far

beyond our natural ability. When they called me to do a TBN special I thought, *Oh, no! What have I got in my closet that will make me look five foot ten? Why can't they call Randi? He has much more confidence than I have. How can I walk into that studio with confidence when I'm really walking with fear and trembling? This is beyond my natural ability.*

Later when David looked at the circumstances, all appeared hopeless. He knew he could not rely on his own strength and ability. Saul was just too jealous. During the times when David ran for his life because Saul pursued him he remembered that little boy who took five smooth stones and killed a giant. He knew he was a good shot—but not *that good*. Even then it was the power of the Spirit and the anointing of God that directed those stones. He knew that limitless power was available to him for any situation— even being pursued by a king.

So Step Over Into the Supernatural

WHEN YOU begin to step into the supernatural, you will never forget it. That's where the giants are defeated. It is something beyond self. It's where God speaks to you and reminds you of the class He wants you to teach, the next place He wants you to minister, the mission trip He wants you to make, the leadership position He wants you to train for, and the gift He wants you to have that's beyond your ability to obtain.

We start by telling the Lord how scared we are. That's a wonderful place to be. Faith is standing on the edge of a cliff, poised on the edge of disaster. If God doesn't come through for you, you are going to fall to your death.

My friend, Pastor Joe Robinson from New Covenant, told me this story one day as I sat in his office doing some radio spots. There was a woman who was trying to break the record for swimming from southern California to Catalina Island. She was the first woman ever to try this. She swam in shark-infested waters while others surrounded her in boats, shooting the sharks in front of her. (If it had been me in that water, the minute they said, "Shark!" I would have been *walking* on the water.) She was surrounded by fog, but everyone, including her mother, kept encouraging her. "Come on, you can make it!"

Often when I need encouragement I'll call Mom. She tells me, "Look up, honey; just keep looking up."

I tell her, "I am, but the birds are pooping on me. It's really bad, and I don't want to look up anymore. I'm tired."

Back to Pastor Joe's story. The swimmer said, "I can't go on; I can't do it." All she could see was the fog around her. Finally she gave up when she thought there was no end to this battle to break a record, and they pulled her out of the water. She was only one-half mile from shore.

Don't Quit Now!

SOMETIMES WE are pressing toward the promise, and we are ready to fall. We have not seen the hand of God move. We have not seen the promise that He has given us come to pass. There has been no change even though we stood and believed, waged war, and prayed. Instead of getting better, things got worse. Do you know that the closer to shore you get, the more the enemy is going to tell you that it's no use and you might as well give up? He will shroud the promise so you can't get a fix on the end in sight.

One dear sister said to me, "Cathy, sometimes you look up and think you see the light at the end of the tunnel, but it's not. It's a train headed straight for you." I thought she was going to tell me the light was the end of my trial. Was she trying to encourage me or what? I'm still wondering.

Don't give up. You are only one-half mile from shore. Don't run from the battle and cast away your hope. Don't cast away your promise. Don't cast away your prophetic word.

Keep swimming. Let me encourage you: You can make it. Wait! There's a shark! Let me kill it for you! Okay! Swim!

Eleven

DON'T GROW WEARY IN WARRING

L ORD, I have done everything there is to do. I confessed, stood, and prayed. What's wrong? Does the Word work or doesn't it? Why isn't this mountain moving?"

Have you ever felt that way? I have good news for you. The Lord is leading us in a season of tremendous spiritual warfare. We can combat the enemy over whom we've already been declared victors! We are breaking bondages and chains of oppression, and the devil hates it. He cannot stand it, and it makes him fighting-mad.

> Finally, be strong in the Lord, and in the strength of His might. Put on the full armor of God, that you may be able to stand firm against the schemes of the devil.
> —EPHESIANS 6:10–11, NAS

One sure thing the devil wants to do is sap you of your

strength. He likes to attack you when you are tired, and when you are tired is *not* the time to get into warfare against him. You must be aware of his schemes because the devil has plans for you.

Some may not believe it, but it is true nonetheless. One day I walked into my Italian grandmother's room and began to pray for her. I said, "I bind the spirit of the devil." Not understanding, she got upset and said, "Don't pray to the devil! You do that, and he'll come after us." I explained to her that I was not praying to him; I was rebuking him. I have found that some people think that if we leave the devil alone, he will leave us alone. But that's not the way it works. It's a myth perpetrated by you-know-who.

The Bible clearly states that we are to know our enemy so we can receive insight into his plots and schemes. Here is a good illustration of this: A young lady went to Vietnam to minister with her family. She approached one of the commanders of the Vietnam War and asked him, "Who are your best soldiers?" She expected him to list the Green Berets, the Rangers, the Navy Seals, or one of the other specialized military groups.

Instead his reply was, "My best troops are those who admit who the enemy is, have tangled with him, and know what he looks like. They have been wounded, sent to hospitals, healed, and returned to the war. They are my best soldiers because they have met the enemy and know his schemes. They are determined never to be wounded in the same place again. They call that the 'Eye of the Tiger.'"

Watch Out for These Attacks!

MOST OF you have been caught by the schemes of the enemy. You've been wounded but returned to the battlefield, healed. When the enemy attacks again, you are prepared. The devil would like for you to go to bed, pull the covers over your head, and be depressed and discouraged. There is an attack against the body of Christ today such as we have not witnessed before this time. The biggest attack used to be fear. Now we can add depression and rejection to the list of the devil's favorite tactics.

If you watch television at all you have seen the commercials that show a gorgeous girl asking you in her sexiest voice to call her on a 900 number if you are lonely and depressed. Of course, it will cost you big bucks because no one can talk for just one minute. And I'll clue you in on something that you probably already know: The girl on the other end of the line *does not look anything like the gorgeous one on television.*

The Lord has been speaking to me and telling me that there is a spirit of loneliness released in the earth today. This spirit not only manifests itself as needing someone to talk to or be with; it causes one to say, "I'm not satisfied in this place so I have to run away," or "I'll change husbands," or perhaps, "I'll go to another church and make new friends." Sometimes it causes people to withdraw into themselves, and because they have been hurt and rejected they won't risk being intimate with anyone else.

It is an outright attack of the enemy. Two can put ten thousand to flight, and the enemy doesn't want you to be in a place where you can agree with anyone to put him in his rightful place. I believe that the strongest, most effective "two" are a husband and wife who come into agreement.

Women have said to me, "That's okay for you, Cathy, but my husband won't pray."

My answer? Take his hand while he's asleep and fake the devil out. Say, "Devil, we are agreeing. Can't you see that our hands are joined together in agreement?"

I was in a service where the pastor had a list of names of powerful men of the city who had come against the church. He lifted the list and said, "Devil, I know you can read, so read this list. You know who you are, so be bound!" I thought that was really cool.

The Lord showed me there is also a demon spirit called "Rama." It means "to come, to knit hearts together in love, to love one another, to make vows with one another, and then leave and stab others in the back on the way out the door." The spirit of Rama means "to betray the covenant." There is a spirit of Rama that has been loosed in the body, and we must stand against it.

There was a situation in my life where I had given and given to friends who were very dear to my heart. All of a sudden I didn't see them anymore. Word came to me that I had failed them. At first I was hurt; then I was just plain mad. I knew what they did was not right. Then I recognized that this situation was representative of a spirit working through the body of Christ, working to separate one from another.

I often ask people in prayer lines where they attend church. Many times the answer I get is, "Well, nowhere really. We are in the Spirit. We just go here and there. We attend several churches in the local area." Sounds like a spiritual cafeteria to me. Just go and take what you want. The enemy doesn't want us to get planted and knit our hearts together. He cannot stand it when we come together with our hearts knitted as one. Why? Because then we can really do warfare against him.

God wants us to stand firm against the schemes of the enemy. His scheme is to separate intimate friends—friends who say, "I'll never separate myself from you. There isn't anything you can ever do that will cause me to throw you away." That's a covenant friendship.

REMEMBER TO DRESS FOR BATTLE

EPHESIANS 6:12 tells us to put on the whole armor of God, "For our struggle is not against flesh and blood, but against the rulers, against the powers, against the world forces of darkness, against the spiritual forces of wickedness in the heavenly places" (NAS).

We have to be wise against Satan's plots. I'm probably not telling you anything you haven't heard over and over again. I'm just chewing it up and spitting it out in a different manner for you. We expect folks in the world to war against us, but it's hard to understand when Christians do it. I have said many times, *I could really serve Jesus great if it weren't for the other Christians.*

The Lord said He is going to rise as a mighty man of war, and He is going to bring His army with Him. We are supposed to be fitting into an army. God has work for us to do, but He also has His work cut out for Him—so many times we have two hundred generals and only five privates.

The Rambos sing a song about shouting down the walls of Jericho called "Shut Up and March." The words tell us to quit talking about our leaders; just shut up and march. Stop disputing over orders; shut up and march. Until you hear the trumpet sound, shut up and march. Instead, what do we do so many times? We sit down and cry.

I can just see the lot of them marching around the walls of Jericho. "I don't want to do this anymore! How come I can't be at the front? Where is Joshua, anyway? I didn't vote for him to be our leader. I wanted my son to head this march." I guess that's why God told this army not to say anything; just shut up and march.

The devil is fighting harder today than ever to try to infiltrate the army of God. We used to sing that old hymn, "Hold the Fort for I Am Coming." As we sang this, all I could see were battered and bruised Christians, bloodied with swollen eyes, teeth knocked out, and the demons marching in upon them, crushing the poor Christians.

Today that's not the picture at all. It's the Christians who are arrayed in splendid battle armor and marching against the gates of hell. That's the way it's supposed to be. One of the battle strategies of Joshua's army was that the Lord told them to sing. I hear some of you saying, "With *my* voice? I could kill the whole enemy army!"

I don't know what they sang. I like to think that it was, "Hallelujah, we won! We have the victory!" I can imagine the enemy on the other side, listening, picking up their stuff and saying as they ran, "We must have lost the war."

You must understand that demons work under authority. Whether in hell or on earth, they can only move on the command of Satan. Like an army, they have strategies to steal, kill, and destroy. There are those that have been assigned to your marriage, household, job, and finances.

The demons that Jesus cast out of the demoniac of Gadara begged Jesus not to send them back to their rulers, because they were fearful, choosing rather to be cast into a herd of swine. During Jesus' ministry on earth He sent out the seventy disciples with the instructions, "Heal the sick, cleanse the lepers, cast out devils." To their amazement they were able to heal the sick, cleanse the lepers, and cast out demons because the demons were subject to them. The disciples returned, absolutely overwhelmed.

AUTHORITY OVER THE ENEMY

JESUS SAID, "And I saw Satan fall like lightning from heaven" (Luke 10:18, NIV). He was not talking about the Garden of Eden. Satan is called the prince of the power of the air (Eph. 2:2). But Jesus said, "When you use My name, you have that same authority that I have given to the seventy when you use the Word of the Lord against the enemy."

The devil is not afraid of Christians who do not pray. The sons of Sceva used the name of Jesus. The demons said, "Jesus I know, and I know about Paul, but who are you?" (Acts 19:14, NIV). Those old boys had no relationship with Jesus.

The devil is not afraid when you say "in the name of Jesus" or when you plead the blood of Jesus if you have no power. But when you have a relationship with Jesus and are a prayer warrior, you put Satan to flight. Clothe yourself in intercessory prayer so you can have the power to fight when the time comes.

The prophetic word alone will not do it for you. You can

be overflowing with "words," but that's not enough. You have to be on an intimate, daily basis with Him if you are going to enter into battle.

The devil knows your weakest link. You must be aware of his battle strategy. You can't always cry out, "Take me home if it's going to be like this." Stand firm.

To be able to stand firm we must know the strategy of the enemy. We often sing the song "It Is Finished." I sang that as a solo about ten years ago. Then I'd come limping in. If there is no more war, then why do I feel like this so often—beat up and bleeding?

Let me illustrate: It means that if my husband were to get into the ring with the heavyweight boxing champion and manage to stand on his feet for half a round, or by some shear coincidence he would knock out the champ, they would give him the coveted belt. I know I don't have anything in my wardrobe that would go with it, but that's beside the point.

They would say, "You are now the world champion, Randi Lechner." They would give him the huge cup with his name engraved on it. Along with these lovely items he would receive a check for ten million dollars. Hallelujah! We could do a lot of ministry with ten million dollars. He'd receive the check, and then he would become the conqueror.

Then with swollen lips, cauliflower ears, and toothless, he would turn to me and say, "Honey, I did it all for *you.*" He would give me the belt, the cup, and the check for ten million dollars. He'd be the conqueror, but because I got the reward, that would mean I was more than a conqueror. There I was, with a gaudy belt, a big metal trophy, and a huge check worth millions, and I didn't even have to get into the ring and get hurt!

WE'RE MORE THAN CONQUERORS

YOU AND I are more than conquerors today because Jesus went the full fifteen rounds with the devil. He knocked him out, took the keys to death, hell, and the grave from him, and He gave those keys to us.

The devil will try to get you to start reasoning: "I tried that but..." "I want to but..." We've got to say, "Yes, the Lord has said it, even though I don't feel like it right now and nothing in me witnesses it, yet I put my trust in His Word." Many Christians live in the soulish realm instead of the Spirit realm. If we object mentally to everything we will have nothing. We say, "Yes, Lord, I know that is true," and "Father, I need Your grace." That is the key. When that happens, we roll up our sleeves and say, "Devil, I'm not taking it anymore. I have the victory!"

The devil doesn't want you mad at him. I'd like to provoke you to be angry at him as if he just came in and stole the baby out of its crib. You say it's not your personality style to get angry. When the Lord told Joshua's army to *shout* the walls of Jericho down, He didn't care if it was their personality style or not. He said, "Shout!" and they shouted. You may shout at the devil with tears streaming down your face, but you will be in a warfare attitude.

The enemy will try to tell you, "There is no hope." Once the Lord was dealing with us to leave our pastorate in Winter Haven, Florida. Right after that our minister of music left, and guess who had to do his job? To top it off, he came back and took his piano from the sanctuary and all we had left to accompany the musicians was an inadequate keyboard on loan from my mother.

The devil started in: "How can you leave *now?* If you do, the whole church will fall apart." He began one accusation after another. Every time we thought we had someone to take over the pastorate, the devil would say, "The church can't even support you; how is it going to support a new pastor if you leave?"

Randi and I began to lose hope because we were beginning to believe the lies of the devil. We started listening to TV ministers who were fighters. They used hype because they believed that what came out of their mouths was what was going to happen. The hype worked, and we got our vision back on line with what God had been speaking to our hearts. The devil wants you to lose your vision to fight. He will then get you to lay down your spirit man. You may still to go church, but you've lost your fight and the devil has won the round.

You've paid too big a price to retreat. He has given you the formula for a solid armor along with power and authority, and you are dressed for battle. Have an attitude that says, "I'm not giving up. I have a promise and I intend to see it fulfilled."

THE WEAPON OF HOPE

IN THE middle of the battle the enemy wants to steal your hope. He would like nothing better than to have you cast all your promises aside. When I was believing for more children I got out all my cassettes with my prophetic promises, and I played them over and over. I wanted to hear the faith and hope as these attributes came boiling up from deep within me. Listening to those tapes worked a work deep within me.

During this time there were wonderful, well-meaning saints who would say to me, "You need to lose seventy-five pounds." So I lost seventy-five pounds—and still no baby. Someone else told me I needed to go on a barley grain diet. I did; still no baby. I was told to lay my desire down on the altar, confess it into being, and many more words of advice. But I knew God would do what He said He would do, all at the appointed time. And He did—six times, but in *His* time, not mine.

Have the attitude that says, "I will not cast away my 'confidence, which has great recompence of reward' (Heb. 10:35). If the enemy can take my hope, then he has everything. Lord, I need Your grace."

I can't count the times my husband has said to me, "Honey, let's get out of the ministry. I cannot take being rejected and hurt anymore. I can't give of myself anymore. I have poured myself into people, paid their electric bills, paid their rent, and put food on their tables. I've clothed their kids, and a month later they are gone, leaving me stabbed in the back." (Have you ever felt that way?)

The Lord always came to our rescue, picked us up, encouraged us, healed us, and put us back on the right track. We just died a little more to self each time—which was the whole idea.

You can walk away a million times, but the grace of God will always bring you back. I sense very strongly that I am speaking right into the heart of someone. You are saying, "I can't take it anymore," but I'm telling you that the grace of God will cause you to rise again. Depression may deflate you, but the anointing of the Spirit of God will inflate you once again.

Put on the whole armor of God right now. Let's talk about a few of the items that compose the whole armor of God as described in the sixth chapter of Ephesians.

GOD'S ARMOR

Put on the whole armour of God, that ye may be able to stand against the wiles of the devil. . . . Stand therefore, having your loins girt about with truth, and having on the breastplate of righteousness; and your feet shod with the preparation of the gospel of peace; above all, taking the shield of faith, wherewith ye shall be able to quench all the fiery darts of the wicked. And take the helmet of salvation, and the sword of the Spirit, which is the word of God.

—EPHESIANS 6:11, 14–17

- *The Breastplate of Righteousness:* If I am righteous, I am just—as if I had never sinned before the Lord. My heart is protected. This piece of armor protects me from every seed of unforgiveness, bitterness, and resentment. Bitterness and resentment will get me nowhere but knarled up with arthritis and will leave me hurt, wounded, and alone. Unforgiveness doesn't hurt anyone but me. Every day I have to come before the Lord and say, "Father, I walk in forgiveness. I forgive them, Lord."

- *The Belt of Truth:* "Father, I thank You that the belt of truth is in my inward parts. I am not a liar; I am not a deceiver. What I say is the Word. Lord, I sow seeds of integrity with my mouth. I will not speak a word that will hurt another person. I've got tongue-control, and the words of my mouth will be pleasing to You."

- *The Sword of the Spirit:* You don't have the authority to go into realms that He has not given you. He has given you authority in the realm where you live; you have authority over your house, your kids, and your family. He has given the church the authority in other areas.

- *The Shield of Faith:* If you can't get anything else for the day, don't forget your shield of faith. The shield of faith protects you and quenches every fiery dart of the enemy.

Did you notice that there is no article of armor to protect your backside? That's because He never expects you to run in retreat. In warring with the enemy our attitude should always be, "Devil, I confuse you and your camp this day. I speak confusion to you and to all your plans for me and my family."

VICTORY!

Twelve

SOMETIMES A SPOONFUL OF SUGAR JUST GIVES YOU WORMS AND MAKES YOU FAT

TRYING to hold a serious conversation with my friend Vonita Goodman was proving to be too difficult. You see, we were returning from an awesome meeting in Philadelphia, and the airline ticket agent had made the horrible mistake of seating us in the middle seats, one row behind the other. From that precarious position we were attempting to discuss what we thought the enemy would do next in order to tempt or deceive us to keep us from the anointing.

"Is it men and sex?" we asked each other over the seats (with men seated on either side of us exchanging fearful glances and looking nervous). We decided that it wasn't. We were way too tired for that. It was hard enough to be sexy with our own husbands. It would take someone like Sean Connery to even get either of us interested—and he's almost a hundred and fifty years old.

Could it be money? There never seems to be enough of it to do everything that is in our hearts to do. It always helps to have more, but God's provision is always more than enough. So we decided money wasn't it either.

We didn't want to run away. We're always traveling, so that wouldn't be any fun. Anyway, I'm not sure the world's beaches are ready for my thighs.

"UNBELIEF!" That's the answer the Holy Spirit spoke to my heart. I was appalled. *Why, that is a "baby" sin,* I thought, horrified. *I am too mature.* I sneered at the very idea!

Again the Holy Spirit whispered, "Unbelief!" That's when I realized that when we stand before Jesus we will not be judged for our sin—Jesus took care of that on the cross— we will be judged for our *unbelief.* Sin is the *fruit;* unbelief is the *root.* For example, when a thief steals, stealing is his fruit. He thinks God will not provide, and that is the root— *unbelief.*

Tears of Regret

As a child I was told that when we stood before the Lord He would wipe away every tear. I was told that meant we were going to be so broken down and depressed by the time Jesus came that He would have to heal us all before He serves dinner.

Now I believe that He will have to wipe away tears of regret for all the unbelief—all the opportunities that were lost due to our lack of trust in His love and provision.

Second Corinthians 5:7 tells us that we walk by faith and not by sight.

There is a super*un*natural attack on your faith in these last days. The enemy's purpose is to rob you of your word, your seed, your purpose, your hope, your inheritance, and your ministry callings.

In Luke 18:8 Jesus asked, "Nevertheless when the Son of man cometh, shall he find faith on the earth?" Is it possible that in the last days the attack on our faith will be so great that Jesus was issuing us a warning? Would subtle adverse circumstances chip away at the believers' resolve to stand "hope against hope" until the answer comes?

With renewed eyes we can read the account of Joshua, Caleb, and the other ten spies in Numbers 13:26–33. In verse 28 the spies wailed, "We saw." Again in verse 32, "We saw." This is the testimony of the natural man who looks to natural things and walks by sight instead of by faith.

"LORD, WE ARE ABLE!"

THE LANGUAGE of unbelief usually is, "We *saw,* but *we are not able."* "We are not strong." "The majority can't be wrong." But the majority was wrong—dead wrong.

Joshua and Caleb "saw" the very same thing, but their report was different from that of the other ten spies. They walked by faith and saw by faith, then they acted by faith.

Beloved, you must determine long before the battle exactly what you believe. If you wait until you are in the middle of the war, it just may be too late.

Joshua and Caleb answered, "The giants are bread for us!" What a contrast to the unbelieving spies who cried, "And we are like grasshoppers in their sight."

The ten spies saw themselves as food to be eaten. Joshua and Caleb saw the Canaanites as food to be *consumed.*

What is the giant you face today? Will it consume you, or will it become bread to feed and strengthen your faith? It is your choice. First *choose,* then *declare your choice!*

"You, marital problem; you, financial crisis; you, church-split; you, cancer, sickness, disease; *you are bread for me!* Mental and emotional instabilities, you are devoured by the word of faith in my mouth!"

It may seem silly and foolish to you, especially if what you see is bigger and louder than the Word and your faith.

I just love Caleb's answer. I can just see his veins bulging in his neck as he states his case before the people. Hands waving, turning furiously to address the crowd, hushing them in order to be heard, he then makes this outrageous and glorious statement: "THE LORD LOVES US!"

That seems trivial and unrelated to the situation the Hebrews were facing at the time, but that is the nuts-and-bolts foundation of faith. "I CAN TRUST HIM BECAUSE HE LOVES ME!"

Because God Loves You

IT IS still the same today. You can trust Him because He loves you. I prophesy to thousands of people every year. The prophetic word the Lord brings is almost always full of His grace, His kindness, and His hope; He has everything under control. That prophetic word is for someone facing a really difficult time *right now*.

The conclusion of faith: We *are* able, for the Lord is with us.

"But the men that went up with him said, We be not able to go up against the people; for they are stronger than we" (Num. 13:31). This is the conclusion of unbelief, which is the result of natural sight when God is left out.

Hopelessness is a condition of godlessness.

"And they brought up an evil report of the land which they had searched unto the children of Israel, saying, The land, through which we have gone to search it, is a land that eateth up the inhabitants thereof; and all the people that we saw in it are men of a great stature" (Num. 13:32). The "evil report" is translated in one version as "the slander of God." I'm not going to slander anyone—but the first person I'm not going to slander is God.

Do Not Accuse Your God

MY PRECIOUS father is dealing with a horrible cancer in his body. What is even worse than the cancer is the devastation of chemotherapy upon his body.

I was lying on the bed next to him, stroking his face,

praying in the Spirit, when a violent wave of nausea hit him. He ran—well, he actually limped—to the bathroom to vomit for the fourth time in one hour. I have never felt such a horrible feeling of helplessness or anger. I silently whispered to God, "My father has done nothing but serve You for the last forty-nine years, and *this* is his reward?" As I opened my mouth to continue my railing, the Lord rebuked me.

"Don't you dare accuse your God!" I apologized to the Lord that day and promised Him I would never again accuse Him.

All unbelief is unreasonable, obstinate, rebellious, prejudiced, presumptuous, insolent, stubborn, boastful, insensible, hardening, and deceitful.

All the miracles the Israelites witnessed did not cure them of unbelief. Neither will miracles today. The agnostics and cynics chalk everything up to coincidence. The health-food people credit alfalfa sprouts, and many Christians invoke the "Lord's sovereign will" dogma.

The disciples saw more miracles than the children of Israel coming out of Egypt, and yet they were still full of unbelief and hardness of heart.

Why is this so bad? Why is unbelief the one thing that stirs God's anger against His people? We get a glimpse into God's heart in Deuteronomy 1:32–33:

> . . . the LORD your God, who went in the way before
> you, to search you out a place to pitch your tents in, in
> fire by night, to shew you by what way ye should go,
> and in a cloud by day.

GOD HAS PREPARED THE WAY

OH, MY precious friend, I wish I could somehow put my arms around you and declare to you, *"Don't be afraid! God has already gone ahead of you to prepare the way!"*

You cannot change the past, but you can sure recreate

the future. The Lord tells us in the very next verse, "And I heard your words." He is listening to your words.

My children never have to worry about what they are going to eat. They never sit around after breakfast obsessing about lunch and dinner. I love them. I would go without to make sure they had food and clothing.

But we slander God when we continue to allow words of doubt, unbelief, and fear to come pouring out of our mouths. It is as wrong to pray about what our God has already promised as it would be an insult to me to hear my children telling their friends they were praying for their dad and me to provide dinner that night and coats to protect them from the cold.

Unbelief Will Hinder Your Miracle

I'VE HEARD various ministers state that they do not believe miracles are for today. I thought to myself, *Well, good, then you won't be disappointed when you don't get one!*

Did they forget to read the part about Abraham? Abraham was an exceptional individual. He was used by Jesus to illustrate the kind of faith that pleases God. There is no guesswork in it.

> No unbelief or distrust made him waver or doubtingly question concerning the promise of God, but he grew strong and was empowered by faith *as he gave praise and glory to God.*
>
> —ROMANS 4:20, AMP, EMPHASIS ADDED

Faith feeds faith. Faith empowered Abraham to even greater levels of faith.

Principle #40,462: The key to waiting for your answer is giving praise and glory to God while you are waiting.

Look around the doctor's office as people are waiting to be seen by him. It's two hours past their appointment. Are they smiling and laughing, giving praise and glory to God while they wait? NO! They are rolling their eyes, slamming down the four-year-old copy of *Highlights* magazine, and reloading their .44 Magnum.

Have you ever seen one person laughing and rejoicing in the grocery line while waiting their turn at the *one* checkout line that is open? Of course not, because they are stuck behind a woman with three grocery carts full of food that won't scan and numerous items in need of price checks. She has in her hand ten zillion coupons while she is yelling at her six children, "Seamus, get off the railing! Shamequa, stop kicking that nice lady who is giving praise and glory to God!"

But take heart! You *can* overcome unbelief. Unbelief is a spirit. Abraham was full of confidence that the Word of God bound Him to fulfill. What he was promised, after twenty-five years of waiting, was fulfilled. He had overcome unbelief by walking by faith. Eventually, unbelief will cut you off from God if you don't overcome it first by faith.

Abraham had his lapses of faith, but God so trusted his inherent integrity that He knew Abraham would trust God no matter what. Regardless of those lapses, Abraham was acknowledged by Him in the Word as a giant of faith and as an example to us today.

This is what God says of Abraham in Genesis 18:19:

> For I know him, that he will command his children and his household after him, and they shall keep the way of the LORD, to do justice and judgment; that the LORD may bring upon Abraham that which he hath spoken of him.

The Lord could fully trust Abraham to follow His Word completely. Can He trust you?

FIRST, TRUST GOD

[Therefore beware,] brethren; take care lest there be in

any one of you a wicked unbelieving heart—which refuses to cleave to, trust in and rely on Him—leading you to turn away and desert or stand aloof from the living God.

—HEBREWS 3:12, AMP

When we begin to distrust the Lord and the keeping of His promises for our lives, we start to reap the very thing we have sown. We get mad at God for not doing what we *wished* would happen, but not what we spoke within range of His hearing. Before we even realize what has happened, anger and bitterness have crept in. We have become another casualty in the body of the Lord Jesus Christ.

Will you give voice to this praise with me? *"Oh, God, You do all things well, and I love You and trust You. I praise You with joy for Your great and glorious master plan being worked out for my life and the lives of the ones I love. Now, let Your rivers of joy flood me and fill me to overflowing as I stay in Your presence."*

BELIEF ACTIVATES FAITH

ONE OF my favorite faith stories is found in Mark 9:23–24. Mark writes about a father who brought his epileptic son to the disciples and asked them to cast out the evil spirit and heal him. They prayed and cast until there was no devil within ten miles, but the son remained the same.

In desperation the father brought his son to Jesus. Out of love for his son he begged Jesus, "Please, Jesus, take pity on my son and heal him." If it had been me that the father had come to, I would have wept at his pitiful story. But not Jesus. His reply, full of compassion, was direct and almost businesslike. *"If thou canst believe, all things are possible to him that believeth."* In other words Jesus was saying, "Dad, it is not pity that activates faith. It is *belief* that activates faith and releases the miracle."

Let's face it; we all know a lot of really pitiful people. They love God, but they go from crisis to crisis with no visible miracles in their lives. Why? Because pity is self-absorbed, whereas it's belief that turns the thoughts and heart toward God.

Jesus was trying to tell this father, "If you want a miracle, you must believe." And the father answered Him with such purity and honesty, "Lord, I believe; help Thou my unbelief." He was saying, "I know You can; I know You will. But there is a little part of my heart that is struggling with what I have 'seen' for so many years. Help me!"

Jesus says, "That's close enough." Then He cast the evil spirit out of the boy and healed him.

BABY STEPS OF FAITH

ONE OF the things I so love about my heavenly Father is that He sees and acknowledges even my baby steps toward faith. I have known Jesus as my Lord and Savior almost all of my life, but I am just now touching the realm of faith that brings miracles.

And so can you. Remember, it begins in your heart and translates to your mind. "As he thinketh in his heart, so is he" (Prov. 23:7). From your mind it will come out of your mouth. Your words will either confirm your faith or betray your unbelief. Also, God is extremely interested in *what you say*. He has warned us that the day will come when we must give an account for idle words.

The Holy Spirit, our gentle reminder—or the "hound of heaven," whichever one you prefer to call Him—will come to assist you.

Fear is a liar. Fear is a spirit. Fear is a spirit without a body looking for a body. If you obey the spirit of fear, fear will come to live in you. You must do and say the opposite of what fear says.

God is not limited in His ability. His ability is connected with His willingness to do for His people. There are no limitations in getting things from God according to His promises.

He has given us power to get wealth (Deut. 8:18) and to

bring power and strength to His people (Ps. 68:33).

And He gave you power in your tongue to bring life where there is death (Prov. 18:21).

Thirteen

ARE WE ALMOST THERE YET?

ANYONE who has ever written—or attempted to write—a book (or for that matter, a letter) knows about opposition. Some call it "writer's block."

Truthfully, I have never encountered such personal warfare, endured such physical attacks, or experienced such a lack of motivation for any project in my life as during the writing of this book. (That is, except for the one time I had to do a report on Robert Frost, the famous composer of "Suwanee River." I got a D on that, and I *still* don't know why.)

The closer I came to finishing the book, the more vicious the attacks became. I never realized the importance of the subject matter for anyone but myself. But now I know!

This book is about inheriting the promise. It's about coming into the place of promise—your own Promised Land in God. If there is anything that the enemy would love to steal from your heart, it is your inheritance. Your inheritance is *everything*.

But Not Without Warfare

ON A cold, gray day in December, I accompanied my mom and dad to the Mayo Clinic in Jacksonville. We were there to get the results from a biopsy my father had undergone the previous day.

We tried to laugh and joke going up on the hospital elevator. I looked around the waiting room. There were so many sick people there. We were ushered into the doctor's office, where I tried messing around with the computer to find information on my dad's report. That's when the doctor came in. "Ha-ha," I joked. He wasn't laughing. I suppose there is really no good way to tell someone they have cancer. We heard him deliver the news—cancer. Afterward the three of us just sat there, numb. My friends may find this hard to believe, but I could not speak. Nothing this awful had ever happened to my family, and I was not prepared.

My poor mother sat beside me in one of those ugly sweatshirts with a hideous picture that a friend had ironed on the front for her birthday. It looked even uglier in the doctor's office. Why hadn't I told her to change before we came here? I looked over at my dad. The doctor was talking . . . blah-blah-blah. *I guess they just have to get used to giving horrible news.* My dad had that look of resignation on his face . . . you know, the one that says, "I'll have the mahogany coffin, please, with the matching satin lining. No, never mind, just throw me off a boat in the Gulf of Mexico." It was awful. And it was my dad's birthday!

Something started rising up within me. *No!* As soon as the doctor took a breath, I started to prophesy the will of God. My mother kept crying, and the doctor sort of fiddled with his pen—as if he were judging the distance from his desk to the door and wondering how close he would actually have to come to me in order to make a break for it.

Cancer. What an awful word. What a *hopeless* word. When you say "cancer," everyone's voice drops real low as they tell you the story of someone who, after a long and horrible bout with the disease, finally (God rest their soul) died. *Everyone*—I mean *everyone*—has one of those stories. So do we. Randi and I lost both his parents to cancer.

On the way home from the clinic I was shouting from the backseat to the devil, to God, to all of Jacksonville, to anyone who would listen. "VICTORY! VICTORY! In Jesus' name, we have victory!" I urged my mom to shout with me, and since she will pretty much do anything I ask her to, she started yelling "victory" with me, sitting there in that ugly sweatshirt and looking totally silly.

My father has always been the conservative, quiet one. He was also the one who had the cancer. But he knew I wouldn't shut up until he started shouting "victory," so he began to shout.

Beloved, the world tells us that we were practicing what is called *denial*. Even the church gets a quiet, hushed tone when someone stands up with a testimony like the one I just shared. But the Word declares, "Shout unto God with the voice of triumph" (Ps. 47:1). God is the Alpha and Omega, the Beginning and the End. He's in charge, even when it's cancer.

"Who's in Denial?"

I WAS relating this story to someone, and they admonished me: "Cathy, your approach is all wrong. The individual needs time to grieve and come to grips with the reality of their disease." I really didn't mean to be obnoxious—not on purpose anyway. However, I got right in this person's face and said, "The reality is *what the Word of God says reality is.* 'I am the God that healeth thee,' and so I am behaving accordingly. We are in the fight for my father's life, and we must determine right now what the battle strategy will be because we *know* the outcome is *victory!"*

"Well, you're in denial. I've worked with a lot of cancer patients over the years; you need to be prepared for death," this person continued—for my own good, of course.

I thanked her kindly and under my breath told her to blow it out of her old wazoo, or something really un-Baptist-like.

We believed Daddy wouldn't get sick from the chemotherapy, but he did. We believed and confessed that he wouldn't lose his hair, but down the shower drain it went. We kept on believing in spite of what we saw. And we saw some wonderful miracles. We were grateful for the little miracles we saw along the way—the absence of mouth sores, his miraculous ability to keep down oatmeal, the return of some of his energy. But most of all, we saw the deepening of my father's walk with God and His intensified work within him.

In All Things, Rejoice

ABOUT A month ago I saw an ad in a Christmas catalog for three wooden, gold-spray-painted letters—JOY. The catalog showed them prominently displayed on a mantlepiece. I have a mantlepiece, so I just had to have them.

When they arrived I decided that instead of sitting the letters on the mantlepiece I wanted to hang them on the wall above. The only catch was that the wooden letters weren't made to be hung on a wall. We tried sticky tape, super glue, and a hot-glue gun. The letters would stay up for a while, but eventually we would hear a crash and find that one of the letters had fallen off the wall.

Most of the problem was with the "J." I decided I would have JOY on my wall—not JO, not OY, not even JY—even if I had to weld the letters into place. The good news is I now have two-foot-high, gold letters spelling JOY over my fireplace. The bad news is that even if an earthquake occurs, I will have JOY on my wall for all of eternity—or until we knock out the wall.

Can I tell you that this is a spiritual lesson? It takes *perseverance* to keep your joy. I have worked long and hard to maintain my walk with God, but from time to time I would inevitably lose my JOY. The "J" would just be sucked right out of the JOY and I would be left with OY. And we both know what that means. When my Jewish husband says, "OY VEY," it usually means, "My God, woman, you are giving me a migraine!"

What a difference the "J" makes. Every time I walk into my family room I start laughing when I think of all the people and all the different devices the Lord has used to keep that JOY level up—even in the midst of tremendous trials.

It is work to keep joy alive. But the good news is that the standard of God is being raised up throughout America because of your defiance of the enemy's tactics and because you have survived this present-day genocide perpetrated by Satan. You see, Satan has systematically planned the destruction of the royal heirs of the latter glory. We are the royal heirs.

We are living in a time when we know God has chosen us to receive a double portion. Dead religion is throwing modesty cloths on ladies who fall "under the power" when they are wearing slacks. We are antagonizers of dead religion, and it's time to kick some major devil-butt!

WE ARE THE ROYAL HEIRS OF CHRIST

IS IT my imagination, or are there more infertile couples than ever before? Is it just chance, or has divorce even among Christians really been on the rise? Is it just the news, or has violent crime become so commonplace that we don't even pay attention unless the murders are sensational? What is going on?

The enemy is out to destroy this generation. Are there more instances of cancer and new, unheard of diseases that have been released today? Yes! This is the generation that will give birth to the greatest pastors, apostles, prophets, teachers, evangelists, missionaries, and psalmists that this world has ever known.

If Satan can get you out of the way, he can get to your kids, your husband, your wife, your parishioners, and your ministry. *You* are the first line of defense, and he knows that with you and your prayers *and* your faith totally in shreds, all he needs to do is walk over you to get to them.

But Satan has not reckoned with the mighty glory of God that has been placed upon our generation.

We are the generation that will be used by God to fill the earth with His glory!

That really makes the enemy mad. We will not give up, we will not cave in, and we will not leave until the promise is fulfilled.

Good News for You and Me

So, what is the outcome of my father's story? He had a demonic visitation, waking him out of a sound sleep. The devil told him that he was going to kill him AND his daughter—ME!

Immediately the presence of the Lord came and ministered to him. He told Dad that the devil is a liar and that no matter what he heard or what he saw, God's Word was true and that HE was in control. The Lord told Dad that we would not die because His hand was upon us. And so we are standing, praising, rejoicing, and growing from faith to faith.

I was reading the Word a few days ago, needing the comfort of His Holy Spirit. The Lord spoke to me out of His Word and said:

> Daughter, there are many who want to know Me in the power of My resurrection. They want the power, the fire, and the glory. But they want to avoid knowing Me in the fellowship of My sufferings. In the power of My

resurrection you stand afar off, but in the fellowship of My sufferings I can draw you close to Me. You have a better understanding of the value of the price I paid with My body on the cross.

I likened it to the lectures I used to get from my parents when I would leave my skates out in the rain and the times I would shrug my parents off when they said I didn't appreciate the things they sacrificed to provide for me. Not until I became a parent and saw the clothes I had lovingly washed and ironed strewn all over my daughter's floor did I fully understand the price my parents paid. When I had my own children I began to pay the price for them.

Properly taught and trained, one day our children will have respect and honor for what we have sacrificially but willingly—at any cost—done for them.

Unless you and I pay the price of waiting patiently, giving glory to God in the midst of our suffering, we can't really know Him.

Jesus paid the greatest price—the loss of everything. He did it in order to give His kids everything. That's us!

● ●
So, please don't give up.
I promise you that it is worth it. He'll keep you in His grace
and in His timing. The promise will come while you still have
the energy and mental faculties to enjoy it! Meantime,
may I offer you some Raisinets? They help. Really!
● ●

Epilogue

TESTIMONIES FROM THE OTHER SIDE

WE ARE constantly bombarded with bad news of what the devil is doing throughout the world. Every news report, radio broadcast, and printed page shouts gloom and doom. If we believed every one of these reports, it would seem that the devil is having his way.

Just so you will know that what I have been writing is not the ravings of a forty-three-year-old housewife who has finally gone over the edge, I'm including the following excerpts from letters that I have received from those who can testify to the power and love of God. Please understand that I am sharing these letters for your encouragement and faith-building—not for any personal glorification. TO GOD BE ALL THE GLORY!

DELIVERANCE FROM REJECTION: My sister-in-law passed your book around to our prayer group....It was not what I expected. I can't explain all the release, revelation, and blessing I have received from reading it. I prayed the prayer for deliverance from the spirit of rejection and cried on my knees before the Lord. . . . I am released. I was dealing with a situation with my son and his wife. . . . I pulled an "Abigail" and saw a beautiful change in both of them immediately. God is awesome! Thank you for the humor with which you have hit home with God's principles.

—*J. S., DELAWARE*

"Faith cometh by hearing...the word" (Rom. 10:17). When God's people hear the living Word, it stimulates even the "tiny seed" of faith in our hearts. This is what we witness time and time again in our ministry. Whether we hear it in person or read from the Bible or a book, it is powerful enough to bring about deliverance, as in this woman's life, or in whatever you need in your case...*today!*

A HAMMER OF CONVICTION: I just read (twice) *I'm Trying to Sit at His Feet, but Who's Going to Cook Dinner?* I just have to tell you what a blessing and challenge that book has been. In your introduction you wrote: "You have not received this book by accident—it's a divine appointment...in answer to your heart's hungry cry." YES! I will bear witness to that...because that's exactly what happened to me.

—*L. W., ALABAMA*

"The steps of a good man are ordered by the LORD" (Ps. 37:23). It never ceases to amaze me how faithful our God is, not only in my life and that of my family, but to the thousands to whom He has so graciously allowed me to minister each year through meetings, conferences, and now through the printed page as well. As Christians we're never "lucky," but we are blessed by an all-seeing, all-caring Father. God, if we will allow Him, will order our lives for our good and

His glory. Many are the times when I think everything is going wrong and that I should be somewhere else rather than where I am at the moment. Then, BAM! I become aware that God has put me there to minister to a certain individual or has placed me in the midst of a circumstance that would become one of the greatest blessings I could have desired. Practice listening to the voice of the Holy Spirit and see if He will not begin to direct your life.

> TRANSFORMED BY THE MESSAGE IN BOOK: My sister-in-law bought your book *I'm Trying to Sit at His Feet, but Who's Going to Cook Dinner?* and passed it around to several ladies in our church. Everyone who has read it has been transformed by the message! I was raised as an Assemblies of God preacher's kid (and still am one) and have experienced a severe amount of rejection. . . . Knowing you are a preacher's kid too really ministered to me. . . . Thank you so much for bringing God's words of healing to me.
>
> —*R. D., California*

Being on the road so much of the year and away from my family and those close to me, I often experience those same terrible feelings of loneliness that so many of you confide in me that you experience. There are the lonely hotel rooms and the numerous times I find myself alone among strangers. David said he encouraged himself in the Lord. At those times I draw comfort from the story Jesus tells about the shepherd who went after the one sheep that was lost. "He searched 'til He found it." How determined He is to search us out, no matter how deep our rejection or misery!

I love this part. When He found that sheep He gently picked it up, put it on His shoulder, and carried it back to the fold. That is just what Jesus does. Can't you just feel the tenderness and warmth of His arms as He cradles you with His healing, loving touch? The rejection and loneliness fade away as you bask in His presence.

BURDEN OF DISCOURAGEMENT LIFTED: I received your book for Christmas from my mother. It was one of those that ministered to my heart....I knew you were planning to come to the Full Gospel Business Men's Association meeting that weekend. I just thought, *I can't go; my son has an all-day basketball tournament....*I did make it just in time. You gave the introduction to the offering. I had a five-dollar bill in my hand and thought, *Oh, that's pretty cheap of me; I'll go to a ten.* I had that thing folded into the smallest square, and then you spoke about how offensive that was to God. I thought, *Okay, God, what do You want?* I got my checkbook out and wrote a one-hundred-dollar check. It was not what I normally would have done. I was under great discouragement....Well, God does great things. After you spoke, I ran into a cousin of mine....Before I knew it, she had me in line to have prayer with you. Standing there I'm thinking, *What am I doing? I don't even know what to ask prayer for.* My feelings were so negative that I didn't know what to ask for. You prayed with me....What a dose of happiness God gave me. A great burden was lifted....I wish I could remember what you prophesied for me....Right now I'm not focusing on just what He said, but that He said it *to me* and gave me a boost when I needed it. Our God is an awesome God! May God bless you....You were used as a stepping stone in my life that day.

—*C. H., ILLINOIS*

PRAYED PRAYER OF SURRENDER: I just finished reading your book *I'm Trying to Sit at His Feet, but Who's Going to Cook Dinner?* I feel I know you as a friend. You have helped me reunite in a deeper surrender to my Lord....This morning I read the prayer of surrender on page 132. I felt a sense of let-go. I physically seemed to be stuck to my sofa, feeling weak from my shoulders to my toes....I found my life and so many answers in your book. You have touched me with the various scriptures and your words....I had to let you know how this book which you have written has truly been a part of my everyday life and how much courage it has instilled in my heart. I have felt total surrender for the first time.

—*M. T., Florida*

There is no more beautiful or heart-touching example of a prayer of surrender than that prayed by Jesus in the garden on the night of His betrayal: "Father, not My will be done, but Thine." He didn't want to drink the cup of suffering, but He surrendered His will to the Father. He drank the cup, despising the shame. He endured the cross and now sits at the right hand of the Father. Like Jesus, we too must surrender if we will sit with Him.

Prophetic Word Received in 1983 Has Come to Pass: I just finished reading your book *I'm Trying to Sit at His Feet, but Who's Going to Cook Dinner?* It helped me so much, especially at this time....The reason I was attracted to your book in the first place is because you gave me a prophecy about fourteen years ago that has taken some time, but every word has come true. (She went on to give a lengthy description of all the prophecies and how God brought each one to pass.) I hope I have encouraged you in your ministry since, in my case, your word from the Lord was right on the mark.

—*C. G., Florida*

"Just as I am, without one plea, but that Thy blood was shed for me." I am often reminded of the words of this beautiful old hymn when I have tried to plan things in my life and get all my ducks in a row. In my mind, everything will now flow smoothly because of my brilliant planning and thought. But you guessed it: That's when everything begins to fall apart and I begin to really get frustrated. "I sought the LORD, and he heard me, and delivered me from all my fears" (Ps. 34:4). What sweet release floods my soul; what joy replaces the desperation. Yes, Lord, I surrender all to Thee.

> THE BOOKS ARE NOT ONLY FOR WOMEN: Sometimes it's so easy to just read books, forgetting that the pages are events in people's lives and the ways the Lord has moved to bring them through. Your two books that my wife purchased have both stirred and encouraged me to have an even greater faith in Jesus and to see Him move in our land.
>
> —*J. R., AUSTRALIA*

> ENCOURAGEMENT FROM MONTHLY MEETINGS IN ORLANDO: I've been attending your meetings steadily....The word of the Lord that you bring each month has encouraged me to continue on the path of righteousness. Actually, there has occurred in me a rising up on the inside to stand against the devil and his schemes that had oftentimes derailed me in the past. Each month the word you share has been confirmation of what the Lord is doing in my heart. It is exactly where I'm at and what my heart is crying out for. I have friends who are unable to attend the meetings due to work or living in another state. Each month I've mailed or given out the tapes from the meetings, and the tapes have impacted their lives as well.
>
> —*V. S., FLORIDA*

One of the greatest and most effective lies of the devil is his "yes, but" lie. He will say, "The Word says....True, but that doesn't apply to you because you are too _____" (you fill in the blank). We have a choice either to believe his lie and receive his rewards (to steal, kill, and destroy) or receive the truth of God's Word and receive life, and that more abundantly.

TAPES MINISTERED TO STUDENT IN COLLEGE: I want to express my thankfulness for your ministry. I was introduced to your ministry a couple of years ago when my mother attended your meetings.... She always sends me copies of the tapes to listen to here at school, and I practically wear them out. I've listened to them over and over again, and I have truly been ministered to by them every time. There are times when I miss my family and need some encouragement, so I pop in one of your tapes and receive from you. Your humor lifts me up, and your bold words challenge me in my walk with the Lord. Thanks again. I know there are probably times when you feel your ministry isn't helping or challenging anyone, but it has and *is* assisting me. I don't think you'll ever know the full effect that your ministry is having on people.... I hope this note encouraged you today.

—*A. M., OKLAHOMA*

HEALED WHILE WATCHING VIDEO: I have so enjoyed your ministry. I heard you...and purchased six tapes and a book.... In July 1996 I was very ill with abdominal problems and facing surgery; a friend brought me one of your videos. It was dynamic! You were praying for the sick and called out "liver and abdominal pain." I felt such warmth and felt God healed me. Since then, no surgery—only God's anointed hand. Praise the Lord!

—*M. O., FLORIDA*

It never ceases to amaze me how faithful the Lord is to honor His Word and inspire faith for people to act upon His promises and receive just what they need. Whether in person or via a tape recorded months earlier, God will use a message for His glory and the building of His kingdom. Let me encourage you, dear reader. If you read a promise from the Lord in this book that touches your spirit, seize it for yourself and let God touch you.

I chuckled at this next letter because the writer, in describing my husband, Randi, said, "Randi just ministered at the church I attend.... *In his shy and introverted style,* Randi encouraged people to read your books. He appeared to grow in height to about seven feet when he spoke about both of your books. I did not quite understand this phenomena; therefore, I purchased both books...."

Now for those of you who know my husband, this is a side of him that I am not familiar with. He is a precious, born-again, completed Jew—but he has never shown me his "shy and introverted style." I really must ask him why he has been hiding this side of his personality from me for the past twenty-one years.

> THE WRITER FURTHER STATES: Since I have a heart for those who unfortunately are called "backsliders," the topics you write about cover many of the issues that confront these baby Christians.... Your book exhorted me to such a point that I definitely will recommend it as suggested reading for all Christians—but especially baby Christians....
>
> —*G. B., CALIFORNIA*

GOD EVEN MINISTERS IN THE AIRPORT: You don't know me, but I feel after reading your books that I know you.... (Someone gave her the book *I'm Trying to Sit at His Feet, but Who's Going to Cook Dinner?*) I stuck it in my briefcase, and as I was sitting in the airport waiting for my plane, I got the book out and started reading it. As I read the introduction, I began to weep. It was as if God had placed your book in my hand at just the right time for a very tired and wounded warrior. And that is why I write—to thank you....I just finished *Couldn't We Just Kill 'em and Tell God They Died?* It was fresh bread for a hungry waiter. It encouraged me and reminded me that my brethren throughout the world are going through the same kind of suffering....You have encouraged me to keep standing in my lentil field.

—*L. L., Florida*

God Fulfills Pregnancy Prophecy: My husband and I went to hear you speak in January of 1997.... That night you called up anyone who was trying to get pregnant. My husband and I went up for prayer. We had been trying to conceive for close to three years. After two unsuccessful fertility drugs and still no pregnancy, we gave up. My husband had little faith left, but I did not. (She told of two other prophecies they received. The letter went on to tell about the first two personal prophecies that came to pass.) On March 7 we found out that I was six weeks pregnant! I would like to thank you for obeying the Holy Spirit. You are a tremendous blessing to us both.

—*N. K., Maine*

Grasping at Straws: I was in the conference this past weekend, and I need to tell you I was grasping at one of my "last straws" when I signed up to come. It would take me a very long time to tell you what these last three years of my life have been like... and to be honest with you, I gave up on God and just crumbled under. I was mad at Him and certainly didn't trust Him anymore. I was just plain sick of life. Broken in a million pieces! How could my loving God allow all this to happen? I just gave up trying to serve a God who would allow so much pain to come into my life.... Cathy, I just wanted you to know you sparked in me—no, you've impregnated me with so much knowledge of *why* this has come to me. I know I am a survivor. It was for the purpose God has in my life that it may be perfected and fulfilled in me. I always had the "head knowledge" of why God allows things to happen, but I had never received the fullness of the "heart knowledge" until I really listened; your teachings sparked a new life in me. . . . God showed me I had "Lot's Wife Syndrome"—always looking back—but thanks to you, I am looking from the center of Crete out on my horizon, and I see a beautiful new SONrise. I haven't arrived yet, but I see the dawn instead of the sunset. . . . Cathy, I just would like to tell you what a blessing you were to me and to tell you I love you for all the sacrifices you make for God to bless His people. I just finished your book and was blessed to my toes by it. . . .

—*S. B., MARYLAND*

King David had been deposed from his throne by his own son—a son who now prepared to go after him and kill his own father! Beyond the Jordan, away from the house of God, David was heartbroken and shattered. He loved his son Absalom more than his own life. He wept and prayed, and something amazing happened. He declared, "I will sing." (See Psalm 61.) Nothing had outwardly changed. His son still sought his life. David was still in the desert. But God touched his heart with faith, and he could sing. Yes, God destroyed his enemy and restored David to the throne, but David learned that he didn't have to wait for it to come to pass *to possess the joy of knowing God was in control and would take care of everything.*

YOU JUST CAN'T OUTGIVE GOD! My heart was fearful and broken before I attended the retreat where you ministered. God set me free when you taught on building a house for God and sowing a seed toward that house. I gave almost all I had from my purse, leaving me with two dollars in gas money to get home. By the time I got home, someone had dropped one hundred ten dollars in my purse; I found it while unpacking my things. . . . Reading your book *I'm Trying to Sit at His Feet, but Who's Going to Cook Dinner?* has filled my husband and me with hope!

—*R. W., PENNSYLVANIA*

God has set certain laws in order in the universe. For instance, there is the immutable law of gravity. We're reminded each time we fly across country that the plane is *defying God's law of gravity.* When something mechanical happens to a plane and it can no longer overcome that law, the law of gravity takes over and the plane crashes to the ground. God also has set in order certain spiritual laws such as the one mentioned in the above letter. He says, "Give, and it shall be given...into *your* bosom" (Luke 6:38, emphasis added). God wants to give unto us, but often we defy His law so He can't bless us.

These are excerpts from just a few of the letters I receive. Yes, I *do* read my mail! I cannot answer every letter, but I enjoy reading the testimonies of God's people. You see, it makes it much easier for me to leave my home, children, and husband when I know that I am going to hurting people who are hungry for the Word of the Lord.

My prayer is that you have gained encouragement from these testimonies of what God *can* and *will* do for His children. He loves you—He *really* does!